Crocheted
Aran
Sweaters

JANE SNEDDEN PEEVER

Martingale®
& COMPANY

To my husband, Todd, for your faith, love, patience, and support; to my two little sweethearts, Tessa and Thomas, for your daily inspiration; and to my mom and dad for your loving encouragement to follow my dreams. Thanks for always believing in me.

CREDITS

President: Nancy J. Martin
CEO: Daniel J. Martin
Publisher: Jane Hamada
Editorial Director: Mary V. Green
Managing Editor: Tina Cook
Technical Editor: Ursula Reikes
Copy Editor: Liz McGehee
Design Director: Stan Green
Cover Design: Stan Green
Illustrator: Laurel Strand

PRODUCED BY THE

SEW 'N TELL STUDIO

EASTON, PENNSYLVANIA

Managing Editor, Acquisitions, and Technical Editor: Susan Huxley
Editorial Assistant and Proofreader: Oli Landwijt
Design and Layout Artist: Barbara Field
Schematics Illustrator: Barbara Field
Cover and Fashion Photographer: J. P. Hamel
Stitch Detail Photographer: Robert Gerheart
Nature Photographer: Barbara Field
Hair and Makeup Artist: Colleen Kubrick
Fashion photography shot at the Harry Packer Mansion in Jim Thorpe, Pennsylvania

Crocheted Aran Sweaters
© 2003 by Jane Snedden Peever

Martingale & Company
20205 144th Ave. NE
Woodinville, WA 98072-8478 USA

www.martingale-pub.com

▍ *Mission Statement*

*Dedicated to providing quality products
and service to inspire creativity.*

Printed in China

08 07 06 05 04 03   8 7 6 5 4 3 2 1

Library of Congress Cataloging-in-Publication Data

Peever, Jane Snedden.
     Crocheted Aran sweaters / Jane Snedden Peever.
          p. cm.
     ISBN 1-56477-484-8
     1. Crocheting—Ireland—Aran Islands—Patterns.
     2. Sweaters—Ireland—Aran Islands. I. Title.
     TT819.I74A726 2003
     746.43'40432—dc21
                                                                2003004861

Contents

Tradition and Innovation

Aran patterns, long celebrated in the knitting world, are now ready for crocheters. In Crocheted Aran Sweaters, *bold texture, old-world tradition, and unexpected colors combine with modern silhouettes to create infinitely wearable cardigans, pullovers, and a vest. You'll find stitch combinations that break new ground, plus the lush cables and patterning that—until now— were mostly in the domain of knitters.*

This book presents sweater designs that will build on your knowledge of the basics, with hopes that you'll learn some fresh and fun techniques as well as expand your crochet skills. You're in for a pleasant surprise: Only 12 stitches, plus a few fundamentals, are all that you need to know to make every sweater in this book. Every one. In fact, you probably already know half of the featured stitches. Whatever type of crocheting you have tried, chances are good that you have worked a bobble, reverse single crochet, spike single crochet, and back or front post double or treble crochet. The remaining stitches in the sweaters are just variations of the ones already mentioned. In any case, you can learn all of them by reviewing the comprehensive instructions and step-by-step illustrations that start on page 74.

There are 23 edgings, panels, and stitch patterns packed into *Crocheted Aran Sweaters*. Every one is explained with very explicit row-by-row and stitch-by-stitch instructions. As you work, you'll know exactly where stitches are placed. For an overview, an explanation of how the stitches and patterns are combined is included in the "Pattern Information" box within each set of sweater instructions. The instructions for the garment pieces even walk you through two of the more challenging aspects of pattern work, which is increasing and decreasing while maintaining a stitch pattern.

Some of the sweaters and vests feature little (or often no) shaping, a single stitch pattern and, perhaps, an edging. These painless patterns are included to introduce beginning crocheters to the joys of Aran stitching. Morning Mist (see page 8) is an excellent first garment. The majority of the sweaters and vests in *Crocheted Aran Sweaters* were designed to look more complex than they really are.

▍ Almost every wrong-side row in every sweater is single crochet.

▍ There's minimal shaping.

▍ Some garment pieces are stitched from side to side so that you can work full rows of single patterns.

▍ A post stitch is often placed at the start of a panel or stitch pattern, so that you don't have to count stitches or mess with stitch markers (unless you like this added security).

▍ Almost every stitch pattern and every yarn works up to the same gauge.

▍ Garment pieces take shape quickly because they're worked in heavier-weight yarns.

▍ Most of the panels and stitch patterns are simple row and stitch repeats.

Crocheted Aran Sweaters has a lot to offer. You can even enjoy the panels and stitch patterns without making an entire sweater. All have been compiled into an encyclopedia, which starts on page 80. Instructions for the panels and stitch patterns are set up so that you can work them into any new project. You can also follow the line-by-line instructions to make a gauge swatch for any sweater that's presented in the book.

Whether traditional or modern, worked as an afghan or a sweater, the beauty of Aran pattern work remains the same. Meandering cables and the many textured patterns can make a flat surface come alive with intertwining textures and twists.

ADVICE FOR CROCHETING ARAN PATTERNS

Aran pattern work is really just a matter of using an assortment of basic stitches in various combinations to produce different effects. You'll be more comfortable with the process when you know a few tricks, become familiar with the featured stitches, and understand how certain stitches are used. The pattern you want to make explains everything in exquisite detail, but the following information will give you an overview of the process.

Top Tips

▍ Maintain two single crochet stitches at each end of every row (except when working ribbing), to simplify shaping.

▍ A turning chain with two or more chains counts as a stitch.

▍ Test your gauge only for stitch patterns that occupy large blocks of the garment piece.

▍ Skip the stitch in the previous row that's behind (or in front of) a post stitch, unless the directions say otherwise.

▍ Use different colored stitch markers to track multiple stitch patterns across a row.

▍ Count the two-chain turning chain as your first post stitch when working ribbing.

▍ Work a half double crochet in the top of the turning chain in the previous row if a post stitch is needed to maintain a stitch pattern.

Learning the Stitches

An experienced crocheter can often tell when work is going awry because the stitches aren't behaving as expected. For example, a post stitch that should be straight is diagonal.

The stitch patterns in this book rely heavily on post stitches. If you're rusty making them, brush up with the instructions in the "Featured Stitches Guide" (see pages 74–80). Pay close attention to illustrations that show the placement of the post stitches. Most crocheters struggle with post stitch patterns because they aren't working around the correct stitch in the row below. The crochet hook is first inserted through the crocheted fabric on the **right** side (not the right side of the work) of the specified stitch (see fig. 20 on page 76).

Crocheted fabric may pucker if you're working the posts too tightly. Finished cables are raised from the surface, but they shouldn't be packed tightly together into a bobble-like puff.

Establishing the Stitch Pattern

Detailed instructions for the panels and stitch patterns are included in the sweater instructions, as well as in the "Pattern Work Encyclopedia."

Abbreviations

alt . . . . . alternate	dc . . . . . . double crochet	inc . . . . . increase(ing)	sl st . . . . . slip stitch
approx . . approximately	dc2tog . . double crochet two stitches together (one stitch decrease)	lp(s) . . . . loop(s)	sp(s) . . . . space(s)
beg . . . . . begin(ning)		pat(s) . . . pattern(s)	ssc . . . . . spike single crochet
blo . . . . . back loop only	dec . . . . . decrease(ing)	rem . . . . remain(s)(ing)	st(s) . . . . stitch(es)
BPDC . . back post double crochet	flo . . . . . . front loop only	rep . . . . . repeat	tch . . . . . turning chain
	foll . . . . . follow(s)(ing)	rnd(s) . . round(s)	TWL . . . twist left
cb2 . . . . . two-stitch cable	FPDC . . front post double crochet	RS . . . . . . right side(s)	tog . . . . . together
cb3 . . . . . three-stitch cable		rsc . . . . . reverse single crochet	TWR . . . twist right
cb4 . . . . . four-stitch cable	FPTR . . . front post treble crochet		tr . . . . . . treble crochet
cr2 . . . . . two-stitch cross		sc . . . . . . single crochet	WS . . . . . wrong side(s)
ch(s) . . . chain(s)	hdc . . . . . half double crochet	sc2tog . . single crochet two stitches together (one stitch decrease)	YO . . . . . yarn over
ch-sp . . . chain-space	hdc2tog . half double crochet two stitches together (one stitch decrease)		
cont . . . . continue(ing)		sk . . . . . . skip	

However, rows may start and end with one or more single crochet stitches. A pattern or panel is worked over a specific number of stitches, which are collectively called the *repeat*. The stitch entry in the encyclopedia identifies the number of stitches in the repeat as the *multiple*.

Sometimes, when you are making the correct width of a garment in your size, the number of stitches across a row results in an incomplete panel or stitch pattern repeat at the end of the rows. In these cases, the stitch pattern is simple enough for you to merely work the last one or two stitches in single crochet. The garment instructions tell you exactly what to do. In some sweater instructions, several single crochet stitches (a border) set up the row so that you only work complete pattern repeats and the design is centered on the garment piece.

A few designs, such as "Cottage Wear" (page 32), require a number of panels or stitch patterns worked in the same row. To help track where each one starts and ends, place a stitch marker at the beginning and end of each stitch pattern. Using different colored stitch markers for each pattern will help you define where each pattern lies within the row and will make it easier to switch from one pattern to the next as you

work. There are instances where stitch markers won't be needed, because front post stitches define the edges of the panel or stitch pattern.

If you don't think you're ready to work multiple panels and stitch patterns across a row, look for a garment that's worked sideways. In other words, the first row is at the side of the garment (or at the center front in a few instances). One edge of the row is at the bottom of the garment and the other edge is at the underarm. As you work subsequent rows, you move toward the center of the garment piece, and increases at the underarm edge build the shoulder.

Shaping the Garment Pieces

Decrease and increase stitches are worked at or near the edges. In some cases, you can work the shaping while maintaining the pattern. When this isn't the case, the stitch pattern repeats are flanked by a border (or selvage) of single crochet stitches. This makes it much easier to work decreases and increases where intricate pattern work is happening.

Working with a textured stitch pattern may seem to get a little tricky when increasing for sleeves and other shaped pieces. An easy way to deal with this is to work the first two stitches and the last two stitches of every row in single crochet. This forms a selvage edge into which simple single crochet increases (2 sc in next st) can be worked. On the next row, the new stitch becomes one of the selvage stitches. If the stitch pattern is simple, you can work a pattern stitch into the third stitch from the beginning and end. You can use this technique for the Crumpled Seed, Mock Cable, Single Pebble, and Single Weave stitch patterns.

Placing a stitch marker at the inside edge of the selvages will help you keep the pattern stitches separate from the selvage stitches. For trickier stitch patterns, keep the stitch markers in their original positions, merely moving them to each new row. It's best to continue working single crochet stitches (thus making the selvage wider and wider) until enough stitches have accumulated to work an entirely new pattern repeat and a two-stitch selvage. Then the stitch markers are moved to the outer edges of the new pattern repeat at the beginning and end of the row, and you start again with a two-stitch selvage.

Decreasing for necklines, sleeve caps, and shoulders can be dealt with in a similar fashion as the increasing, by working the first and last two stitches of every row in single crochet. A simple single crochet decrease (sc2tog) can be worked within these edges. Place a stitch marker after the first two single crochet stitches and before the last two single crochet stitches to keep the pattern separate from the selvage.

As the stitch markers are moved inward to accommodate the decreasing number of stitches in the row, you need to maintain the two-stitch selvage. In other words, you work a new single crochet, rather than maintaining the established pattern repeat, at the second and second-to-last stitches in every row. You can use this technique for the Crumpled Seed, Mock Cable, Single Pebble, and Single Weave stitch patterns.

For trickier stitch patterns, move the stitch markers one complete repeat in from the selvage stitches. Now work the outside stitches in single crochet until they are consumed by the decreases.

Common Phrases

▌ **Across:** Continue stitching up to—but not including—the stitch noted after "to."

▌ **As; As for; Work as for:** Follow the referenced instructions to stitch the new row or garment piece.

▌ **Current row:** The row-in-progress.

▌ **First stitch:** The first stitch in the row, closest to the right edge when working from right to left and quite often replaced by a turning chain.

▌ **In st pat as established:** Maintain the stitch pattern that already exists in previous rows and stitches.

▌ **In st pat:** Work in the specified combination of rows and stitches as detailed in the referenced pattern.

▌ **Multiple of:** Number of stitches in a pattern repeat.

▌ **Move marker:** Remove stitch marker from next stitch, make new stitch in marked stitch, and place marker in new stitch.

▌ **Next stitch:** The stitch in the previous or earlier row, immediately beside the one that was just made in the current row.

▌ **Pattern repeat:** Combination of rows and/or stitches that are continued in sequence.

▌ **Place marker:** Attach stitch marker to specified stitch or stitch just worked.

▌ **Previous row:** The most recently finished row.

▌ **Row below:** The second row underneath the row-in-progress.

▌ **To end:** Continue stitching until row is completed.

▌ **Turning chain:** One or more chain stitches at the beginning of a row that help "turn" the work and raise the hook to the height of the new row.

▌ **Two rows below:** The third row below the row-in-progress.

▌ **Work as for . . . to:** Stitch the new row or garment piece, following the referenced instructions, up to—but not including—the step, row, or section noted after "to."

▌ **Work even:** Stitch across rows and/or make more rows without decreasing or increasing the number of stitches.

Morning Mist

Snuggle into a soft turtleneck when overcast skies get you down. Soft yarn and simple stitches yield a garment that drapes beautifully and isn't too stiff for comfort.

▌ *Featured Stitch Patterns*

Double Posts and Ridges . . . . *see page 84*
Post Rib . . . . *see "Cuff," steps 11–13, on page 12*

▌ *Supplies*

H/8 (5 mm) crochet hook
4 stitch markers

▌ *Gauge*

14 sts and 18 rows to 4" in Double Posts and Ridges stitch pattern

▌ *Sizing and Finished Sweater Measurements*

	EXTRA SMALL	SMALL	MEDIUM	LARGE	EXTRA LARGE
TO FIT BUST	31½"	34¼"	37¼"	41"	43¼"
FINISHED BUST	36½"	40½"	43"	47"	48½"
SHOULDER LENGTH	5¾"	6½"	7"	8"	8¼"
SLEEVE LENGTH*	18½"	18½"	19"	19"	19½"
CENTER BACK LENGTH	24½"	25"	26"	27"	28"

Measurement with cuff folded back to final position.

▌ *Yarn Requirements*

PLYMOUTH *ENCORE* #233 LIGHT LAVENDER	EXTRA SMALL	SMALL	MEDIUM	LARGE	EXTRA LARGE
	8 balls	9 balls	9 balls	10 balls	11 balls

This is the best sweater to make if you're just learning to crochet or want to practice post stitches. The body is only two basic stitches—single crochet and front post double crochet—with a basic ribbing added for the luxurious fold-back cuffs and turtleneck collar. The front and back are both worked from the bottom up and later stitched together at the sides. The collar is crocheted on after the front and back are sewn together at one shoulder. The sleeve starts at the wrist, with edge increases to make the piece wide enough for the upper arm. Since the cuffs are added after the sleeve is completed, you can adjust the length for a perfect fit.

BACK

1 Ch 65 (72, 76, 83, 86).

Foundation Row: Sc in 2nd ch from hook (count as 1 st) and in each ch to end, turn. [64 (71, 75, 82, 85) sts]

2 Row 2 (WS): Ch 1 (do not count as st), sc in first and each st to end, turn.

3 Row 3: Ch 1 (do not count as st), sc blo in each of first 1 (1, 3, 3, 1) sts, place marker for start of Double Posts and Ridges st pat, sc blo in each of first 2 sts, *FPDC around each of next 2 sts in row below (foundation row), sc blo in each of next 5 sts*, rep from * to * across to last 5 sts, FPDC around each of next 2 sts in row below, sc blo in each of next 3 sts, place marker (Medium and Large only), sc blo in each of next 0 (0, 2, 2, 0) sts, turn.

Note: The FPDC, a post stitch, is worked into an earlier row. This leaves the corresponding st in the previous row unworked (see fig. 22 on page 76). Do not make a stitch into it and do not count it as a stitch unless the instructions indicate otherwise.

4 Row 4 and All WS Rows: Ch 1 (do not count as st), sc in first and each st to end, turn.

Row 5: Ch 1 (do not count as st), sc blo in first and each st to marker, move marker, sc blo in each of first 2 sts, *FPDC around each of next 2 FPDC in row below, sc blo in each of next 5 sts*, rep from * to * across to 5 sts before marker, FPDC around each of next 2 FPDC in row below, sc blo in next 3 sts, move marker (if necessary for your size), sc blo in next 0 (0, 2, 2, 0) sts (to end of row), turn.

Double Posts and Ridges st pat established.

5 Cont in Double Posts and Ridges st pat as established (rep step 4, rows 4–5), moving markers to current row (if necessary for your size), until 24½ (25, 26, 27, 28)" from beg. Fasten off.

FRONT

1 Work as for back, until 22 (22½, 23¼, 24¼, 25)" from beg, ending with WS row completed. Remove 2nd marker.

Left Neck Shaping

2 Next Row (Dec Row; RS): Ch 1 (do not count as st), sc blo in first and each st to marker, move marker, sc blo in each of first 2 sts, *FPDC around each of next 2 FPDC in row below, sc blo in each of next 5 sts*, rep from * to * 2 (3, 3, 3, 3) more times, FPDC around each of next 2 (0, 0, 2, 2) FPDC two rows below, sc blo in next 2 (0, 0, 1, 4) sts, turn. Rem sts unworked. [28 (31, 33, 36, 37) sts]

3 Next Row (Dec Row; WS): Ch 1 (do not count as st), sc2tog, sc in next and each st to end, turn. [27 (30, 32, 35, 36) sts]

Next Row (Dec Row): Ch 1 (do not count as st), sc blo in first and each st to marker, work in pat as established across to last 3 sts, sc blo in next st, sc2tog, turn. [26 (29, 31, 34, 35) sts]

4 Rep step 3 (last 2 rows) 3 more times. [20 (23, 25, 28, 29) sts]

5 Work even in st pat as established until 24½ (25, 26, 27, 28)" from beg. Fasten off.

Right Neck Shaping

6 With RS of front facing, working into last full-width row and starting at inner edge of left neck shaping, sk next 8 (9, 9, 10, 11) sts.

Next Row (RS): Join yarn with sc (count as st) in next unworked st, sc blo in first 2 sts, cont in st pat as established to end of row, turn. [28 (31, 33, 36, 37) sts]

7 Next Row (Dec Row): Ch 1 (do not count as st), sc in first and each st to last 2 sts, sc2tog, turn. [27 (30, 32, 35, 36) sts]

Next Row (Dec Row): Ch 1 (do not count as st), sc2tog, sc blo in next st, work in pat as established to end, turn. [26 (29, 31, 34, 35) sts]

8 Rep step 7 (last 2 rows) 3 more times. [20 (23, 25, 28, 29) sts]

9 Work even in st pat as established until 24½ (25, 26, 27, 28)" from beg. Fasten off.

SLEEVE (Make 2)

1 Ch 36.

Foundation Row: Sc in 2nd ch from hook (count as st) and in each ch to end, turn. [35 sts]

2 Row 2: Ch 1 (do not count as st), sc in first and each st to end, turn.

3 Row 3 (RS): Ch 1 (do not count as st), sc blo in each of first 2 sts, *FPDC around each of next 2 sts in row below (foundation row), sc blo in each of next 5 sts*, rep from * to * across to last 5 sts, FPDC around each of next 2 sts in row below, place marker, sc blo in each of next 3 sts, turn.

4 Row 4: Ch 1 (do not count as st), sc in first and each st to end, turn.

5 Row 5: Ch 1 (do not count as st), sc blo in first 2 sts, *FPDC around each of next 2 FPDC in row below, sc blo in each of next 5 sts*, rep from * to * across to last 5 sts, FPDC around each of next 2 FPDC in row below, sc blo in each st to end, turn.

Double Posts and Ridges st pat established.

6 Row 6 (Inc Row): Ch 1 (do not count as st), 2 sc in first st, sc in next st, place marker, sc in next and each st to last 5 sts, place marker, sc in next and each st to last st, 2 sc in last st, turn. [37 sts]

7 Row 7: Ch 1 (do not count as st), sc blo in first and each st to marker, move marker, *FPDC around each of next 2 FPDC in row below, sc blo in each of next 5 sts*, rep from * to * across to marker, move marker, FPDC around each of next 2 FPDC in row below, sc blo in each st to end, turn.

Row 8: Ch 1 (do not count as st), sc in first and each st to end, moving markers as encountered, turn.

Row 9: As row 7.

Row 10 (Inc Row): Ch 1 (do not count as st), 2 sc in first st, sc in next and each st to marker, move marker, sc in next and each st to marker, move marker, sc in next and each st to last st, 2 sc in last st, turn. [39 sts]

Cuff

10 With RS of sleeve facing, work along wrist edge of sleeve as follows:

Foundation Row: Join yarn with sc in bottom corner (count as st), sc in each ch of base ch to end, turn. [35 sc]

11 Row 2: Ch 3 (count as dc), dc in next and each sc to end, turn. [35 dc]

12 Row 3: Ch 2 (count as st), BPDC around next st (2nd st from edge), *FPDC around next st, BPDC around next st*, rep from * to * across to last st, hdc in last st (top of tch), turn.

Row 4: Ch 2 (count as hdc), FPDC around next st, *BPDC around next st, FPDC around next st*, rep from * to * across to last st, hdc in last st (top of ch-2 tch), turn.

Post Rib st pat established.

13 Work even in pat as established (rep step 12, last 2 rows) until 6" from beg. Fasten off.

COLLAR

1 With right sides together, sew front to back at right shoulder. (See page 92 for seaming options.)

2 Place marker on back at inner edge of left shoulder 5¾ (6½, 7, 8, 8¼)" from outer edge, to mark neck.

3 Unfold front and back at right shoulder seam. With RS facing, join yarn to front with sc (count as 1 st) at inner edge of left front shoulder.

Foundation Row: Work evenly spaced sc along neck edge to marker on back, turn. Finish with odd number of sts. Remove markers.

4 As steps 11 and 12 of Cuff.

5 Work even in Post Rib st pat as established until 6" from beg. Fasten off.

8 Rep step 7 (last 4 rows) 14 (14, 15, 16, 17) more times, working new Double Posts and Ridges st pat rep in sc every time 7 sts are accumulated between beg (or end) edge and marker. [67 (67, 69, 71, 73) sts]

9 Work even in st pat as established until 15½ (15½, 16, 16, 16½)" from beg. Fasten off.

FINISHING

1 If necessary, block all of the garment pieces (see page 92).

2 Sew back to front at left shoulder. (See page 92 for seaming options.)

3 With WS together and starting at neck, sew collar edges together for 2½".

4 Turn sweater inside out. With collar RS together, finish joining collar edges. Turn sweater RS out again. When collar is folded to its final position, the seam line will not be visible.

5 On front and back, place marker at each side (vertical edge) 9½ (9½, 9¾, 10, 10½)" below shoulder seam.

6 Sew sleeves into body between markers and then sew side and underarm sleeves. Do not join cuff edges.

7 With WS together, join cuff edges in same manner that the collar was seamed, as explained in steps 3 and 4 of Finishing, on this page.

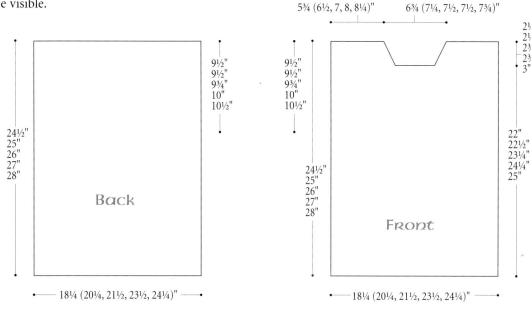

Back

9½"
9½"
9¾"
10"
10½"

24½"
25"
26"
27"
28"

18¼ (20¼, 21½, 23½, 24¼)"

5¾ (6½, 7, 8, 8¼)"   6¾ (7¼, 7½, 7½, 7¾)"

2½"
2½"
2¾"
2¾"
3"

9½"
9½"
9¾"
10"
10½"

24½"
25"
26"
27"
28"

22"
22½"
23¼"
24¼"
25"

Front

18¼ (20¼, 21½, 23½, 24¼)"

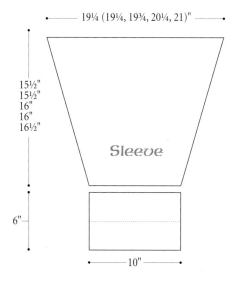

19¼ (19¼, 19¾, 20¼, 21)"

15½"
15½"
16"
16"
16½"

Sleeve

6"

10"

Rugged Rover

The hills beckon. Respond wearing a go-anywhere zippered jacket that's worked in a sturdy yarn made with wool from the harsh eastern coast of Canada.

▌ *Featured Stitch Patterns*

Crumpled Seed . . . . *see page 83*
Herringbone Cable . . . . *see page 85*
Post Rib . . . . *see "Hood Band," steps 3–5, on page 18*

▌ *Supplies*

7 (4.5 mm) crochet hook
H/8 (5 mm) crochet hook
20 (20, 22, 22, 22)" or 50 (50, 56, 56, 56) cm separating zipper*
All-purpose sewing thread, color matched to yarn
Hand-sewing needle
Quilter's straight pins (1¼" long, with large head)
Stitch marker
Buy your zipper after assembling the garment pieces so you'll know the exact length that you need.

▌ *Gauge*

14 sts and 16 rows to 4" in Crumpled Seed stitch pattern with H/8 (5 mm) hook
14 sts and 15 rows to 4" in sweater pattern with H/8 (5 mm) hook

▌ *Sizing and Finished Sweater Measurements*

	EXTRA SMALL	SMALL	MEDIUM	LARGE	EXTRA LARGE
TO FIT BUST	31½"	34¼"	37¼"	41"	43¼"
FINISHED BUST	38"	40"	43"	47"	49"
SHOULDER LENGTH	5"	5½"	5¾"	6¾"	6¾"
SLEEVE LENGTH	18"	18½"	18½"	19"	19½"
CENTER BACK LENGTH	22½"	22½"	23"	23½"	24"

▌ *Yarn Requirements*

BRIGGS AND LITTLE *HERITAGE* #42 BLUE HEATHER	EXTRA SMALL	SMALL	MEDIUM	LARGE	EXTRA LARGE
	9 balls	9 balls	10 balls	11 balls	11 balls

The sweater back and fronts are worked sideways, featuring a herringbone stitch pattern flanked by rows of basic stitching. The combination works out to a 15-row repeat. The sleeves and hood, made with alternating slip and single crochet stitches (the Crumpled Seed stitch pattern), are worked from bottom to top. The chart that follows summarizes the repeat.

▮ *Sweater Pattern Summary*

SWEATER REPEAT ROW	FEATURED STITCH OR STITCH PATTERN	SEE PAGE
1–6	Herringbone Cable st pat rows 2–7	85
7–8	Single crochet stitch	
9	Slip stitch	
10	Single crochet stitch	
11–14	Crumpled Seed st pat rows 2–3 worked twice	83
15	Slip st	

BACK

Worked sideways from left to right.

1 With larger hook, ch 74 (74, 76, 78, 80).

Foundation Row: Sc in 2nd ch from hook (count as st) and each ch to end, turn. [73 (73, 75, 77, 79) sts]

2 Row 2 (WS): Ch 1 (do not count as st), sc in first and each st to end, turn.

3 Row 3: Ch 1 (do not count as st), sc in each of first 3 sts, *ch 1, sk next st, sc in next st*, rep from * to * to end, turn.

Herringbone Cable st pat established.

4 Rows 4–7: As rows 4–7 of Herringbone Cable st pat (see page 85).

5 Rows 8–9: Ch 1 (do not count as st), sc in first and each st to end, turn.

6 Row 10: Ch 1 (do not count as st), sl st in first and each st to end, turn.

7 Row 11: Ch 1 (do not count as st), sc in first and each sl st to end, turn.

8 Row 12: Ch 1 (do not count as st), sc in first st, *sl st **loosely** in next st, sc in next st*, rep from * to * to end, turn.

Row 13 (RS): Ch 1 (do not count as st), sc in first and each st to end, turn.

Crumpled Seed st pat established.

9 Rows 14 and 15: Rep step 8 (last 2 rows) once.

10 Row 16: Ch 1 (do not count as st), sl st in first and each st to end, turn.

Sweater pat 15-row rep established.

11 Work even in sweater pat as established, starting with Herringbone Cable st pat, until 19 (20, 21½, 23½, 24½)" from beg. Fasten off.

RIGHT FRONT

Worked from side to center front.

1 With larger hook, ch 74 (74, 76, 78, 80).

Foundation Row: Sc in 2nd ch from hook (count as st) and each ch to end, turn. [73 (73, 75, 77, 79) sts]

2 Beg st pat according to "Sweater Pattern Summary" chart, starting with Sweater Repeat row 11 (9, 7, 3, 1).

3 Work even in sweater pat as established until 5 (5½, 5¾, 6¾, 6¾)" from beg, ending with WS row completed.

Right Neck Shaping

4 Cont in pat as established, shape as follows:

Next Row (Dec Row; RS): Ch 1 (do not count as st), work in st pat as established across to last 6 sts, sc2tog, turn. Rem sts unworked. [68 (68, 70, 72, 74) sts]

5 Next Row (WS): Work even in sweater pat as established, turn.

Next Row (Dec Row; RS): Ch 1 (do not count as st), work in st pat as established across to last 2 sts, sc2tog, turn. [67 (67, 69, 71, 73) sts]

6 Rep step 5 (last 2 rows) 4 more times. [63 (63, 65, 67, 69) sts]

7 Work even in st pat as established until 9½ (10, 10¾, 11¾, 12¼)" from beg. Fasten off.

LEFT FRONT

Worked sideways from center front to side.

1 With larger hook, ch 64 (64, 66, 68, 70).

Foundation Row: Sc in 2nd ch from hook (count as st) and each ch to end, turn. [63 (63, 65, 67, 69) sts]

Left Neck Shaping

2 Beg st pat according to "Sweater Pattern Summary" (see page 16), starting with row 8.

3 Cont even in sweater pat as established until 1½ (1½, 2, 2, 2½)" from beg, ending with WS row completed.

4 Next Row (Inc Row; RS): Ch 1 (do not count as st), work in st pat as established across to last st, 2 sc in last st, turn. [64 (64, 66, 68, 70) sts]

Next Row: Ch 1 (do not count as st), work in st pat as established to end, turn.

5 Rep step 4 (last 2 rows) 4 more times. [68 (68, 70, 72, 74) sts]

6 Next Row (Inc row; RS): Ch 1 (do not count as st), work in st pat as established across to last st, 2 sc in last st, ch 5, turn. [69 (69, 71, 73, 75) sts + 5 chs]

7 Next Row (Inc Row; WS): Sc in 2nd ch from hook (count as st) and each of next 3 chs, work in st pat as established to end, turn. [73 (73, 75, 77, 79) sts]

8 Work even in sweater pat as established until 9½ (10, 10¾, 11¾, 12¼)" from beg. Fasten off.

SLEEVE *(Make 2)*

Worked from wrist to shoulder.

1 With larger hook, ch 36.

Foundation Row: Sc in 2nd ch from hook (count as st) and each ch to end, turn. [35 sts]

2 Row 2 (WS): Ch 1 (do not count as st), sc in first st, *sl st **loosely** in next st, sc in next st*, rep from * to * to end, turn.

3 Row 3: Ch 1 (do not count as st), sc in first and each st to end, turn. Crumpled Seed st pat established.

4 Row 4 (Inc Row): Ch 1 (do not count as st), 2 sc in first st, *sl st **loosely** in next st, sc in next st*, rep from * to * across to last 2 sts, sl st in next st, 2 sc in last st, turn. [37 sts]

5 Row 5: Rep step 3 (row 3).

6 Row 6: Rep step 2 (row 2).

7 Row 7 (Inc Row): Ch 1 (do not count as st), 2 sc in first st, work in pat as established across to last st, 2 sc in last st, turn. [39 sts]

Work even in st pat as established for 2 rows.

8 Rep step 7 (last 3 rows) 12 (14, 14, 16, 17) more times. [63 (67, 67, 71, 73) sts]

9 Work even in st pat as established until 16½ (17, 17, 17½, 18)" from beg. Fasten off.

ASSEMBLY

If necessary, block all garment pieces. Sew front to back at shoulders and sides. (See page 92.)

HOOD

1 With smaller hook and RS facing, join yarn with sc in top corner of neck at right front.

Foundation Row: Work evenly spaced sc around neck to top corner of left front, turn. Finish with an odd number of sts, placing sts farther apart for a loose neckline or closer for a snugger fit.

2 Row 2 (WS): Ch 1 (do not count as st), sc in first st, *sl st in next st, sc in next st*, rep from * to * to end, turn.

Row 3: Ch 1 (do not count as st), sc in first and each st to end, turn. Crumpled Seed st pat established.

3 Rep step 2 (last 2 rows) until 12 (12, 12½, 12½, 13)" from beg, ending with WS row completed. Place marker in center st.

Side 1 Hood Shaping

4 Next Row (Dec Row; RS): Work in Crumpled Seed st pat as established to 2 sts before marker, sc2tog, remove marker, turn. Rem sts unworked.

5 Next Row (Dec Row): Ch 1 (do not count as st), sc2tog, work in Crumpled Seed st pat as established to end, turn.

Next Row (Dec Row): Ch 1 (do not count as st), work in Crumpled Seed st pat as established across to last 2 sts, sc2tog, turn.

6 Rep step 5 (last 2 rows) 2 more times. Fasten off.

Side 2 Hood Shaping

7 Beg with RS facing, work into last full-width row and start at inner edge of Side 1 Hood Shaping as follows:

Foundation Row: Join yarn with sc in first available st (count as st), sc2tog, work in Crumpled Seed st pat as established on full-width row to end, turn.

8 Next Row (Dec Row): Ch 1 (do not count as st), work in st pat as established across to last 2 sts, sc2tog, turn.

Next Row (Dec Row): Ch 1 (do not count as st), sc2tog, work in st pat to end, turn.

9 Rep step 8 (last 2 rows) 2 more times. Fasten off.

HOOD BAND

1 Sew top and shaped edges.

2 Join yarn with sc (count as st) in corner of neck at right front, work around front edge of hood to corner of neck at left front as follows:

3 Foundation Row: Working with smaller hook and RS facing, sc in end of each row. Finish with an odd number of stitches.

4 Row 2: Ch 3 (count as st), dc in next and each st to end, turn.

5 Row 3: Ch 2 (count as hdc), FPDC around next st (2nd st from edge), *BPDC around next st, FPDC around next st*, rep from * to * across to last st, hdc in last st (top of ch-3 tch), turn.

6 Row 4: Ch 2 (count as hdc), BPDC around next st, *FPDC around next st, BPDC around next st*, rep from * to * across to last st, hdc in last st (top of ch-2 tch), turn. Fasten off.

BOTTOM BAND

1 Join yarn with sc (count as st) in lower corner of left front and work around lower edge to lower right front corner as follows:

2 Next Rows: As steps 3–6 of Hood Band.

CUFF

1 Join yarn with sc (count as st) in lower corner at narrowest edge of sleeve and work across narrowest edge as follows:

2 Next Rows: As steps 3–6 of Hood Band.

FINISHING

Sew bottom band edges together. Sew underarm of each sleeve. Sew sleeves into body.

ZIPPER

1 With zipper closed, place RS of tape against WS of opening on a front. Align bottom of zipper with lower edge of bottom band. Let top of zipper extend ½" into hood opening. Join with quilter's pins.

2 With needle and thread, backstitch to front.

3 Place second front, RS up, on top of rem side of zipper. Pin every few inches.

4 Open zipper and backstitch tape to front.

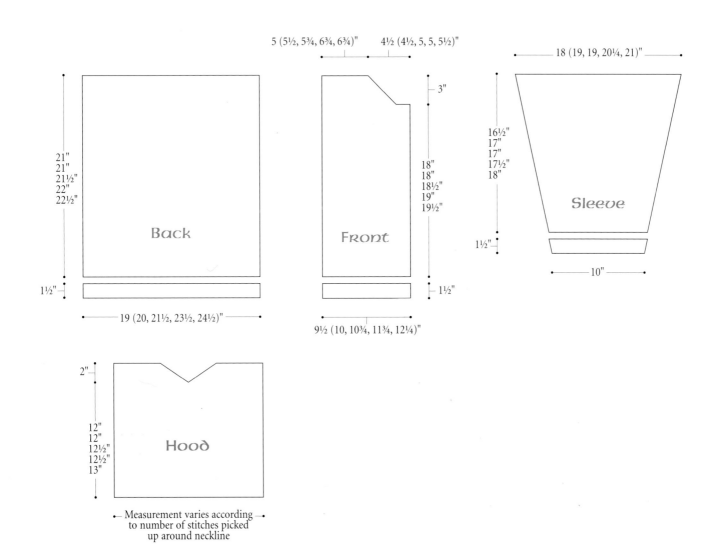

Dusty Miller

Echoing the sweet lilt of a Scottish folk song, post stitches dance up and down a classic cardigan silhouette.

▌ *Featured Stitch Patterns*

Mock Cable . . . . *see page 87*
Mock Post Rib . . . . *see "Collar," steps 2–5, on page 24*
Zigzag Posts . . . . *see page 91*

▌ *Supplies*

7 (4.5 mm) crochet hook
H/8 (5 mm) crochet hook
6 buttons, ⅝" (1.5 cm) diameter
6 stitch markers

▌ *Gauge*

14 sts and 18 rows to 4" in Zigzag Posts stitch pattern
  with H/8 (5 mm) hook

▌ *Sizing and Finished Sweater Measurements*

	EXTRA SMALL	SMALL	MEDIUM	LARGE	EXTRA LARGE
TO FIT BUST	31½"	34¼"	37¼"	41"	43¼"
FINISHED BUST*	36"	38½"	42"	46"	48"
SHOULDER LENGTH	6"	6"	7"	7½"	8"
SLEEVE LENGTH	19"	19½"	19½"	20"	20"
CENTER BACK LENGTH	25¾"	26¼"	27½"	28"	29¾"

Measurement of buttoned garment.

▌ *Yarn Requirements*

	EXTRA SMALL	SMALL	MEDIUM	LARGE	EXTRA LARGE
LION BRAND *WOOL-EASE* #099 FISHERMAN	8 balls	8 balls	9 balls	10 balls	11 balls

Despite appearances to the contrary, the cardigan pieces feature only two patterns and little more than basic stitches plus the front post double crochet. Since the pieces are worked from side to side, the stitch patterns are worked one at a time. To make a front, for example, one edge of a row is at the bottom band and the opposite edge is at the shoulder.

BACK

Worked sideways from left side to right side.

1 With larger hook, ch 86 (88, 92, 94, 100).

Foundation Row: Sc in 2nd ch from hook (count as st) and each ch to end, turn. [85 (87, 91, 93, 99) sts]

2 Row 2 (RS): Ch 1 (do not count as st), sc in each of first 2 (4, 0, 2, 0) sts, place marker, sc in next st, *ch 1, sk next st, sc in each of next 7 sts*, rep from * to * across to last 2 sts, ch 1, sk next st, sc in last st, turn.

Zigzag Posts st pat and sc edge stitches established.

3 Rows 3–7: Work even in pat as established (start with row 3 of Zigzag Posts st pat; see page 91) between marker and shoulder edge, cont sc border sts, moving marker to current row.

Stitch Pattern Change

4 Row 8: Ch 1 (do not count as st), sc in first and each st to end, moving markers, turn.

5 Row 9: Ch 1 (do not count as st), sl st **loosely** in first and each st to end, turn.

Beg of Mock Cable pat established.

6 Rows 10–15: Work even in Mock Cable st pat as established (starting with row 4; see page 87).

Stitch Pattern Change

7 Rows 16–21: Work even in Zigzag Posts st pat (starting with row 2; see page 91) between marker and opposite edge, cont border sts in single crochet and move marker to current row.

Work even in Mock Cable st pat (starting with row 2; see page 87) for 8 rows.

8 Rep step 7 (last 14 rows) until 18 (19½, 21, 23, 24)" from beg. Fasten off.

Note: Length from beg of work is width of garment.

RIGHT FRONT

Worked sideways from right side to center front.

1 Work as for Back until 6 (6, 7, 7½, 8)" from beg, ending with WS row completed.

Right Shoulder Shaping

Cont 14-row sweater pat rep as established, **at same time** shape armhole as follows:

2 Next Row (Dec Row; RS): Ch 1 (do not count as st), work in pat as established across to last 4 (4, 5, 5, 6) sts, sc2tog, turn. Rem 2 (2, 3, 3, 4) sts unworked. [82 (84, 87, 89, 94) sts]

Note: If working the Zigzag Posts st pat in step 2 row, dec may interfere with pat rep at end of row. After completing last possible full, eight-st rep near end of row, work sc border sts to complete row.

3 Row (Dec Row): Ch 1 (do not count as st), sc2tog, work in pat as established to end, turn. [81 (83, 86, 88, 93) sts]

Next Row (Dec Row): Ch 1 (do not count as st), work in pat as established across to last 2 sts, sc2tog, turn. [80 (82, 85, 87, 92) sts]

4 Rep step 3 (last 2 rows) 3 more times. [74 (76, 79, 81, 86) sts]

5 Work even in 14-row sweater pat as established until 9 (9½, 10½, 11½, 12)" from beg. Fasten off.

LEFT FRONT

Worked sideways from left side to center front.

1 Work as for Back until 6 (6, 7, 7½, 8)" from beg, ending with WS row completed.

Left Shoulder Shaping

Cont 14-row sweater pat rep as established, **at same time** shape armhole as follows:

2 **Next Row (Dec Row; RS):** Sl st in first 2 (2, 3, 3, 4) sts, ch 1 (do not count as st), sc2tog, work in pat as established to end, turn. [82 (84, 87, 89, 94) sts]

3 **Next Row (Dec Row):** Ch 1 (do not count as st), work in pat as established across to last 2 sts, sc2tog, turn. [81 (83, 86, 88, 93) sts]

Next Row (Dec Row): Ch 1 (do not count as st), sc2tog, work in pat as established to end, turn. [80 (82, 85, 87, 92) sts]

4 Rep step 3 (last 2 rows) 3 more times. [74 (76, 79, 81, 86) sts]

5 Work even in 14-row sweater pat as established until 9 (9½, 10½, 11½, 12)" from beg. Fasten off.

SLEEVE *(Make 2)*

Worked sideways, from underarm to underarm.

1 With larger hook, ch 22 (24, 24, 26, 26).

Foundation Row: Sc in 2nd ch from hook (count as st) and each ch to end, turn. [21 (23, 23, 25, 25) sts]

First Side Shaping

2 **Row 2 (Inc Row; RS):** Ch 1 (count as st), sc in next st *ch 1, sk next st, sc in each of next 7 sts*, rep from * to * across to last 4 (6, 6, 8, 8) sts, ch 1, sk next st, sc in next st, place marker, sc in next and each st to last st, 2 sc in last st, ch 4, turn. [22 (24, 24, 26, 26) sts + 4 chs]

Row 3: Sc in 2nd ch from hook (count as st) and in each of next 2 chs, move marker, sc in next and each st and ch-sp to end of row, turn. [25 (27, 27, 29, 29) sts]

Zigzag Posts st pat established between markers, with sc border sts outside markers. Cont shaping as follows, starting with row 4 of Zigzag Posts st pat (see page 91):

3 **Row 4 (Inc Row; RS):** Work in pat as established to marker (if enough sts are now available to work another pat rep, remove marker, work pat rep, place marker) sc in each st to last st, 2 sc in last st, ch 4, turn. [26 (28, 28, 30, 30) sts + 4 chs]

Row 5: Sc in 2nd ch from hook (count as st) and in each of next ch and sc to marker, move marker, work in pat as established to end of row, turn. [29 (31, 31, 33, 33) sts]

4 Rep step 3 (last 2 rows) 8 more times, **at same time** cont 14-row sweater pat rep by completing first rep of Zigzag Posts st pat, then alternating with Mock Cable st pat reps. [61 (63, 63, 65, 65) sts]

5 Work even in sweater pat as established until 14 (14½, 14½, 15, 15)" from beg, ending with WS row completed. Edge without shaping is top of sleeve.

Second Side Shaping

Cont 14-row sweater pat rep as established, alternating single reps of Mock Cable and Zigzag Posts st pats, while shaping as follows:

6 **Next Row (Dec Row; RS):** Ch 1 (do not count as st), work in pat as established across to last 4 sts, sc2tog, turn. Rem 2 sts unworked. [58 (60, 60, 62, 62) sts]

Next Row (Dec Row): Ch 1 (do not count as st), sc2tog, work in pat as established to end, turn. [57 (59, 59, 61, 61) sts]

7 Rep step 6 (last 2 rows) 9 more times. [21 (23, 23, 25, 25) sts]

8 Work even 1 row in pat as established. Fasten off.

2 Row 2 (WS): Ch 1 (do not count as st), sc in next and each st to end, turn.

3 Row 3 (RS): Ch 1 (do not count as st), sc in first st, *FPDC around next sc in row below, sc in next st*, rep from * to * to end, turn.

Mock Post Rib st pat established.

4 Row 4: Ch 1 (do not count as st), sc in first and each st to end, turn.

Row 5: Ch 1 (do not count as st), sc in first st, *FPDC around FPDC in row below, sc in next st*, rep from * to * to end, turn.

5 Rep step 4 (rows 4 and 5). Fasten off.

BOTTOM BAND

1 Work with smaller hook and RS facing.

Foundation Row: Join yarn with sc in lower corner of left front (count as st), work evenly spaced sc around lower edge to lower corner of right front, turn. Finish with odd number of sts.

2 As steps 2–5 of Collar. Fasten off.

LEFT FRONT BAND

1 Work with smaller hook and RS facing.

Foundation Row: Join yarn with sc (count as st) in top corner of collar at left front neck, work evenly spaced sc down left front edge to lower corner of bottom band, turn. Finish with odd number of sts.

2 As steps 2–5 of Collar. Fasten off.

RIGHT FRONT BAND

1 Mark buttonholes on right front with evenly spaced markers, placing first buttonhole 1" below upper corner of front and last buttonhole 1" above lower edge of bottom band.

2 Work with smaller hook and RS facing.

ASSEMBLY

1 If necessary, block all garment pieces (see page 92).

2 Sew back to front at shoulders and side seams.

COLLAR

1 Work with smaller hook and RS facing.

Foundation Row: Join yarn with sc (count as st) in top corner of right front neck, work evenly spaced sc around neck to top corner of left front, turn. Finish with odd number of sts.

Foundation Row: Join yarn with sc (count as st) in lower corner of right front bottom band, work evenly spaced sc up right front edge to top corner of collar, turn. Finish with odd number of sts.

3 Row 2 (WS): Ch 1 (do not count as st), sc in each st to end, turn.

4 Row 3 (RS): Ch 1 (do not count as st), sc in first st, *FPDC around next sc in row below, sc in next st*, rep from * to * across to first marker, ch 3 (buttonhole made), **cont in st pat as established to next marker, make buttonhole**, rep from ** to ** to last buttonhole made, cont in st pat to end, turn.

5 Row 4: Ch 1 (do not count as st), sc in first and each sc and ch to end, turn.

Row 5: Ch 1 (do not count as st), sc in first st, *FPDC around FPDC in row below, sc in next st*, rep from * to * to end.

6 Rep step 5 (rows 4 and 5). Fasten off.

7 Sew buttons on left front.

CUFF

1 With smaller hook and RS facing, work across narrowest edge of sleeve as follows:

Foundation Row: Join yarn with sc in lower corner, work evenly spaced sc in end of rows to end, turn. Finish with odd number of sts.

2 As steps 2–5 of Collar. Fasten off.

3 Make cuff for rem sleeve in same manner.

FINISHING

Sew underarm seam on each sleeve. Sew sleeves into body. (See page 92 for seaming options.)

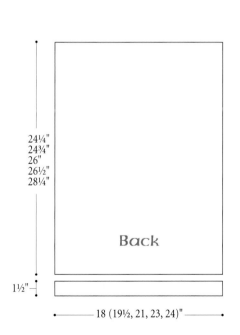

24¼"
24¾"
26"
26½"
28¼"

Back

1½"

18 (19½, 21, 23, 24)"

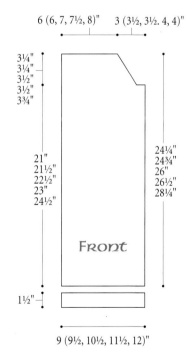

6 (6, 7, 7½, 8)"   3 (3½, 3½. 4, 4)"

3¼"
3¼"
3½"
3½"
3¾"

21"
21½"
22½"
23"
24½"

24¼"
24¾"
26"
26½"
28¼"

Front

1½"

9 (9½, 10½, 11½, 12)"

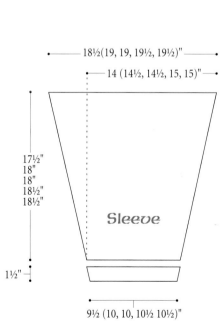

18½(19, 19, 19½, 19½)"

14 (14½, 14½, 15, 15)"

17½"
18"
18"
18½"
18½"

Sleeve

1½"

9½ (10, 10, 10½ 10½)"

Ivy League

Learn the ropes of Aran stitching without tackling an ambitious project. In the Aran tradition, cables, which represent fishermen's ropes, give way to a simply stitched vest back.

▌ *Featured Panel and Stitch Patterns*

Two-Row Cable . . . . *see page 89*
Rope Diamond . . . . *see page 88*
Crumpled Seed . . . . *see page 83*
Single Pebble . . . . *see "Body Edging," steps 2–3, on page 31*

▌ *Supplies*

7 (4.5 mm) crochet hook
H/8 (5 mm) crochet hook
4 stitch markers
4 buttons, ½" (1.2 cm) diameter

▌ *Gauge*

14 sts and 16 rows to 4" in Rope Diamond panel with H/8 (5 mm) hook
14 sts and 18 rows to 4" in Crumpled Seed st pat with H/8 (5 mm) hook

▌ *Sizing and Finished Sweater Measurements*

	EXTRA SMALL	SMALL	MEDIUM	LARGE	EXTRA LARGE
TO FIT BUST	31½"	34¼"	37¼"	41"	43¼"
FINISHED BUST	32¼"	34½"	38"	42"	45½"
SHOULDER LENGTH	2½"	3"	3"	4"	4½"
CENTER BACK LENGTH	17"	17½"	18"	18½"	19"

▌ *Yarn Requirements*

SKACEL *SNOW GOOSE* #3005 ARAN	EXTRA SMALL	SMALL	MEDIUM	LARGE	EXTRA LARGE
	4 balls	4 balls	5 balls	5 balls	6 balls

This is the perfect opportunity to learn to combine multiple stitch patterns. Three identical cables flank a central motif. The process is thoroughly explained in the instructions and, once the cable repeats are established, the work is straightforward. The back is worked entirely in alternating single crochet and slip stitches.

▌ Vest Pattern Summary for Front

VEST ROW	ROPE DIAMOND PANEL ROW	CABLES 1 AND 3 ROW	CABLE 2 ROW
6	6	—	—
7	7	—	—
8	8	—	—
9	9	—	—
10	10	—	—
11	11	—	—
12	12	—	2
13	13	—	3
14	14	2	4
15	15	3	5
16	16	4	6
17	17	5	5
18	18	6	6
19	19	5	5
20	20	6	6
Next rows	Rep 7–20	Rep 5–6	Rep 5–6

BACK

1 With larger hook, ch 58 (62, 68, 74, 80).

Foundation Row: Sc in 2nd ch from hook and in each ch to end, turn. [57 (61, 67, 73, 79) sts]

2 Row 2 (WS): Ch 1 (do not count as st), sc in first st, *sl st **loosely** in next st, sc in next st*, rep from * to * to end, turn.

Row 3 (RS): Ch 1 (do not count as st), sc in first and each st to end, turn.

Crumpled Seed st pat established.

3 Work even in st pat as established (rep step 2; last 2 rows) until 9 (9, 9½, 9½, 10)" from beg, ending with WS row completed.

Shoulder Shaping

4 Next Row (Dec Row, RS): Work in Crumpled Seed st pat as established across to last 4 sts, turn. Rem sts unworked. [53 (57, 63, 69, 75) sts]

5 Rep step 4 (last row) once more. [49 (53, 59, 65, 71) sts]

6 Next Row (Dec Row, RS): Ch 1 (do not count as st), sc2tog, work in st pat as established across to last 2 sts, sc2tog, turn. [47 (51, 57, 63, 69) sts]

7 Rep step 6 (last row) 5 (6, 8, 8, 9) more times. [37 (39, 41, 47, 51) sts]

8 Work even in st pat as established until 16½ (17, 17½, 18, 18½)". Fasten off.

LEFT FRONT

1 With larger hook, ch 2.

Foundation Row (WS): Work 3 sc in 2nd ch from hook, turn. [3 sts]

2 Row 2 (Inc Row): Ch 1 (do not count as st), 2 sc in first sc, ch 1, sk next sc, 2 sc in last sc, turn. [5 sts]

3 Row 3 (Inc Row): Ch 1 (do not count as st), 2 sc in first sc, sc in next and each st and ch-1 sp to last st, 2 sc in last sc, turn. [7 sts]

4 Row 4 (Inc Row): Ch 1 (do not count as st), 2 sc in first sc, working in front of work make 4 dc in skipped st in row 2, in previous row sk 4 sc behind 4 dc just worked, sc in next st, 2 sc in last st, turn. [9 sts]

5 Row 5 (Inc Row): As row 3. [11 sts]

6 Row 6 (Inc Row): Ch 1 (do not count as st), 2 sc in first st, sc in next st, TWR, cb2, TWL, sc in each of next 2 sts, 2 sc in last st, turn. [13 sts]

7 Row 7 (Inc Row): Ch 1, sc in first and each st to last st, 2 sc in last st, turn. [14 sts]

Rope Diamond panel established.

8 Row 8 (Inc Row); Side Border: Ch 1 (do not count as st), 2 sc in first st;

Rope Diamond: Sc in next 2 sts, TWR , sc in next st, cb2, sc in next st, TWL, sc in each of next 2 sts, (Rope Diamond panel row 8 worked; see page 87);

Front Border: Work 2 sc in last st, turn. [16 sts]

9 Row 9 (Inc Row): Ch 1 (do not count as st), sc in first and each st to last st, 2 sc in last st, turn. [17 sts]

10 Row 10 (Inc Row); Side Border: Ch 1 (do not count as st), 2 sc in first st, sc in each of next 2 sts;

Rope Diamond: Sc in next st, TWR, sc in each of next 2 sts, cb2, sc in each of next 2 sts, TWL, sc in next st;

Front Border: Sc in next st, 2 sc in last st, turn. [19 sts]

Side Shaping

11 Row 11 (Inc Row): Ch 1 (do not count as st), sc in first and each st to last st, 2 sc in last st, ch 6 (8, 11, 15, 18), turn. [20 sts + 6 (8, 11, 15, 18) ch]

12 Row 12 (Inc Row); Side Border: Sc in 2nd ch from hook (count as st) and in each of next 4 (6, 9, 13, 16) chs;

Cable 2 Setup: Sc in each of next 2 sts, ch 1, sk next st, sc in next 2 sts;

Rope Diamond: Sc in next st, TWL, sc in each of next 2 sts, cb2, sc in each of next 2 sts, TWR, sc in next st;

Front Border: Sc in each of next 2 sts, 2 sc in last st, turn. [26 (28, 31, 35, 38) sts]

13 Row 13: Ch 1 (do not count as st), sc in each st and ch-sp to end, turn.

14 Row 14; Side Border: Ch 1 (do not count as st), sc in each of first 0 (2, 5, 9, 12) sts;

Cable 1 Setup: Sc in each of next 2 sts, ch 1, sk next st, sc in each of next 2 sts;

Cable 2: Sc in next st, working in front of work make 3 dc in skipped st in row below, sk 3 sc behind 3 dc just made, sc in next st;

Rope Diamond: Sc in each of next 2 sts, TWL, sc in next st, cb2, sc in next st, TWR, sc in each of next 2 sts;

Cable 3 Setup: Sc in each of next 2 sts, ch 1, sk next st, 2 sc in last st. [27 (29, 32, 36, 39) sts]

15 Row 15: Ch 1 (do not count as st), sc in next and each sc and ch-sp to end, turn.

16 Row 16 (Inc Row); Side Border: Ch 1 (do not count as st), sc in each of first 0 (2, 5, 9, 12) sts;

Cable 1: Sc in next st, working in front of work make 3 dc in skipped st in row below, sk 3 sc behind 3 dc just made, sc in next st;

Cable 2: Sc in next st, cb3, sc in next st;

Rope Diamond: Sc in each of first 3 sts, TWL, cb2, TWR, sc in each of next 3 sts;

Cable 3: Sc in next st, working in front of work make 3 dc in skipped st in row below, sk 3 sc behind 3 dc just made, 2 sc in last st, place marker, turn. [28 (30, 33, 37, 40) sts]

17 Row 17: Ch 1 (do not count as st), sc in first and each st to end, turn.

18 Row 18; Side Border: Ch 1 (do not count as st), sc in each of first 0 (2, 5, 9, 12) sts;

Cable 1: Sc in next st, cb3, sc in next st;

Cable 2: Sc in next st, cb3, sc in next st;

Rope Diamond: Sc in next 4 sts, sk next 3 FPDC, FPTR around next FPDC, (sk sc in current row behind FPTR just made), sc in each of next 2 sc, working in front of FPTR just made, FPTR around first skipped FPDC (sk sc in current row behind FPTR just made), sc in each of next 4 sts;

Cable 3: Sc in next st, cb3, sc in last 2 sts, turn.

19 As shown in the "Vest Pattern Summary for Front," cont in vest pat as established, starting with row 5 of Two-Row Cable st pat (see page 89) and row 19 of Rope Diamond panel (see page 88), **at same time** maintain side border by working sc in each of first 0 (2, 5, 9, 12) sts every RS row. Work even until 7 (7, 7½, 7½, 8)" from first stitch marker, ending with RS row completed.

Left Shoulder Shaping

20 Next Row (Dec Row; WS): Ch 1 (do not count as st), sc2tog, work in st pats as established to end, turn. [27 (29, 32, 36, 39) sts]

Work even in st pats as established for 3 rows.

21 Rep step 20 once more. [26 (28, 31, 35, 38) sts]

When dec interferes with pat rep for cables (starting with cable 3), complete each with the finishing row. (See Two-Row Cable st pat "Finishing Row" on page 89.)

22 Next Row (Dec Row; WS): Ch 1 (do not count as st), sc2tog, work in st pats as established across to last 4 sts, turn. Rem sts unworked. [21 (23, 26, 30, 33) sts]

23 Next Row (Dec Row): Ch 1 (do not count as st), sc2tog, work in st pats as established to end, turn. [20 (22, 25, 29, 32) sts]

Next Row (Dec Row): Ch 1 (do not count as st), work in st pats as established across to last 2 sts, sc2tog, turn. [19 (21, 24, 28, 31) sts]

Next Row (Dec Row): Ch 1 (do not count as st), sc2tog, work in st pats as established to end, turn. [18 (20, 23, 27, 30) sts]

Next Row (Dec Row): Ch 1 (do not count as st), sc2tog, work in st pats as established across to last 2 sts, sc2tog, turn. [16 (18, 21, 25, 28) sts]

24 Rep step 23 until 14 (15, 15, 19, 21) sts rem.

Note: Stop at desired stitch count, even if you don't complete all rows in step 23.

25 Cont in Rope Diamond panel as established, working armhole edge even and cont dec 1 st every 4th row at neck edge until 9 (11, 12, 15, 16) sts rem.

26 Work even in st pat as established until 16½ (17, 17½, 18, 18½)", from beg of side seam. Fasten off.

RIGHT FRONT

1 Work as for Left Front to step 8.

2 As for Left Front steps 9 and 10 except reverse shaping by working Front Border, Rope Diamond, and then Side Border. [19 sts]

Side Shaping

3 Row 11 (Inc Row): Ch 6 (8, 11, 15, 18), turn, sc in 2nd ch from hook (count as st) and in each ch, 2 sc in next st, sc in next and each st to end, turn. [25 (27, 30, 34, 37) sts]

4 Row 12 (Inc Row); Front Border: Ch 1 (do not count as st), 2 sc in first st, sc in each of next 2 sts;

Rope Diamond: Sc in next st, TWL, sc in each of next 2 sts, cb2, sc in each of next 2 sts, TWR, sc in next st;

Cable 2 Setup: Sc in each of next 2 sts, ch 1, sk next st, sc in each st to end, turn. [26 (28, 31, 35, 38) sts]

5 As for Left Front to Left Neck Shaping, except reverse shaping by working Front Border, Cable 3, Rope Diamond, Cable 2, Cable 1, and Side Border. [19 sts]

Right Shoulder Shaping

6 Next Row (Dec Row; WS): Ch 1 (do not count as st), work in st pats as established across to last 2 sts, sc2tog, turn. [27 (29, 32, 36, 39) sts]

Work even in st pats as established for 3 rows.

7 Rep step 6 once more. [26 (28, 31, 35, 38) sts]

When dec interferes with pat rep for cables (starting with cable 3), complete each with the finishing row. (See Two-Row Cable st pat "Finishing Row" on page 89.)

8 Next Row (Dec Row; WS): Ch 1 (do not count as st), sl st in first 4 sts, work in st pats as established across to last 2 sts, sc2tog, turn. [21 (23, 26, 30, 33) sts]

9 Next Row (Dec Row): Ch 1 (do not count as st), work in st pats as established across to last 2 sts, sc2tog, turn. [20 (22, 25, 29, 32) sts]

Next Row (Dec Row): Ch 1 (do not count as st), sc2tog, work in st pats as established to end, turn. [19 (21, 24, 28, 31) sts]

Next Row (Dec Row): Ch 1 (do not count as st), work in st pats across to last 2 sts, sc2tog, turn. [18 (20, 23, 27, 30) sts]

Next Row (Dec Row): Ch 1 (do not count as st), sc2tog, work in st pats as established across to last 2 sts, sc2tog, turn. [16 (18, 21, 25, 28) sts]

10 Rep step 9 until 14 (15, 15, 19, 21) sts rem.

Note: Stop at specified st count, even if you don't complete all rows in step 9.

11 Cont in Rope Diamond panel as established, working armhole edge even and cont dec 1 st every 4th row at neck edge until 9 (11, 12, 15, 16) sts rem.

12 Work even in panel as established until 16½ (17, 17½, 18, 18½)", from beg of side seam edge. Fasten off.

FINISHING

Sew back to front at shoulders. Sew side seams. (See page 92 for seaming options.)

BODY EDGING

1 Mark evenly spaced buttonholes on right front, placing first buttonhole ¼" below beg of neck shaping and last 1" above bottom edge of bottom band.

2 Foundation Row: With smaller hook and RS facing, join yarn with sc in bottom edge at left side seam. Work evenly spaced sc around entire outer edge of garment, working ch-1 and skipping 1 st to create buttonhole at each of the four stitch markers on right front edge, turn.

3 Row 2 (WS): Ch 1 (do not count as st), sc in first st, *hdc in next st, sl st **loosely** in next st*, rep from * to * across to last 2 sts, hdc in next st, sc in last st. Fasten off.

4 Sew buttons on left front.

ARMHOLE EDGING

1 Foundation Row: With smaller hook and RS facing, join yarn with sc at side seam, work evenly spaced sc in row ends around armhole edge, turn.

2 As Body Edging step 3.

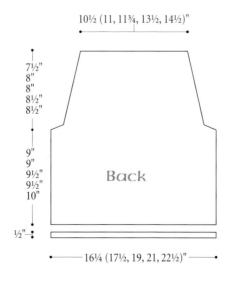

10½ (11, 11¾, 13½, 14½)"

7½"
8"
8"
8½"
8½"

9"
9"
9½"
9½"
10"

Back

½"

16¼ (17½, 19, 21, 22½)"

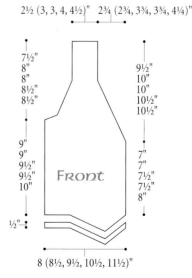

2½ (3, 3, 4, 4½)"   2¾ (2¾, 3¾, 3¾, 4¼)"

7½"
8"
8"
8½"
8½"

9½"
10"
10"
10½"
10½"

9"
9"
9½"
9½"
10"

Front

7"
7"
7½"
7½"
8"

½"

8 (8½, 9½, 10½, 11½)"

31

Cottage Wear

Warm up and dress down for a weekend of fun in the country. A classic you'll cherish for many years, this pullover is well worth the time you spend stitching it.

▌ *Featured Panels and Stitch Patterns*

▌ *Supplies*

7 (4.5 mm) crochet hook
H/8 (5 mm) crochet hook
2 stitch markers

▌ *Gauge*

15 sts and 18 rows to 4" in Crumpled Seed stitch pattern with H/8 (5 mm) hook

▌ *Sizing and Finished Sweater Measurements*

	EXTRA SMALL	SMALL	MEDIUM	LARGE	EXTRA LARGE
TO FIT BUST	31½"	34¼"	37¼"	41"	43¼"
FINISHED BUST	37½"	39½"	42"	46"	50"
SHOULDER AND SLEEVE LENGTH	25"	25¾"	26¼"	26¾"	27¾"
CENTER BACK LENGTH	23½"	23¾"	24¼"	25¼"	26¼"

▌ *Yarn Requirements*

	EXTRA SMALL	SMALL	MEDIUM	LARGE	EXTRA LARGE
PATONS *CLASSIC WOOL* #214 DUSKY BLUE	7 balls	8 balls	8 balls	9 balls	10 balls

Pattern Information

The highlight of this sweater is the central panel of interlocking diamonds on the body. Flanking this are Blossoms panels that are worked over a different number of rows than the main stitch pattern (see figs. 1 and 2). You can read up on the stitch patterns—or make a gauge swatch—by referring to the row-by-row guidance in the "Pattern Work Encyclopedia." Since the back and front are worked from bottom to top, you'll need to pay close attention to changing stitch patterns as you work across each row. To ease this process, you can track the rows with the "Sweater Pattern Summary," at right.

Raglan shaping and a V-neck increase the complexity of the work. Working two single crochet stitches at each shaped armhole and sleeve edge produces a decorative seam when the garment pieces are whipstitched together with the wrong side facing.

Easy-stitch borders add up to no-fuss shaping because increases and decreases can be made with little attention to maintaining the stitch pattern. All of the garment pieces begin with the ribbing, then the work is pivoted so that you make the first row of the rest of the shape by working into the ends of the rows of ribbing.

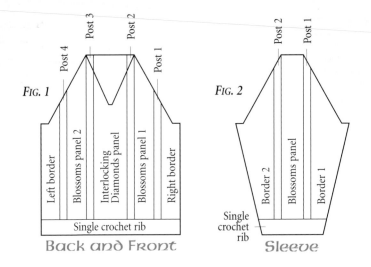

FIG. 1 — Back and Front

FIG. 2 — Sleeve

▌ *Sweater Pattern Summary*

SWEATER REPEAT ROW	BLOSSOMS PANEL ROW	INTERLOCKING DIAMONDS PANEL ROW	CRUMPLED SEED STITCH PATTERN ROW	POST ROW ACTION
1	1	1	1	sc
2	2	2	2	sc
3	3	3	3	FPDC
4	4	4	2	sc
5	5	5	3	FPDC
6	6	6	2	sc
7	7	7	3	FPDC
8	8	8	2	sc
9	9	9	3	FPDC
10	10	10	2	sc
11	2	11	3	FPDC
12	3	12	2	sc
13	4	13	3	FPDC
14	5	14	2	sc
15	6	15	3	FPDC
16	7	16	2	sc
17	8	17	3	FPDC
18	9	18	2	sc
19	10	19	3	FPDC
Next rows 2–10	4–19	2–3		sc then FPDC

34

BACK

Body worked along ribbing edge.

Ribbing

1 With smaller hook, ch 10.

Foundation Row: Sc in 2nd ch from hook and in each ch to end, turn. [9 sc]

2 Row 2: Ch 1 (do not count as st), sc blo in first and each st to end, turn.

Single Crochet Rib st pat established.

3 Work even in st pat (rep step 2, row 2) for 68 (72, 76, 84, 92) more rows.

Body

4 With larger hook, pivot to work across one long edge of ribbing as follows:

Row 1 (RS): Ch 1 (do not count as st), sc in end of each row, turn. [70 (74, 78, 86, 94) sts]

5 Row 2; Left Border and Post 4 Setup: Ch 1 (do not count as st), sc in first st, *sl st loosely in next st, sc in next st*, rep from * to * across next 8 (10, 12, 16, 20) sts, sc in next st, (Crumpled Seed st pat established), sc in each of next 2 sts (Post 4 established);

Panels and Posts Setup: Sc in each of next 42 sts;

Post 1 and Right Border Setup: Sc in each of next 2 sts, (Post 1 established), sc in next st, *sl st in next st, sc in next st*, rep from * to * across to last st (seed st pat established), sc in last st, turn.

6 Row 3; Right Border: Ch 1 (do not count as st), sc in first 12 (14, 16, 20, 24) sts, FPDC around each of next 2 sts in row below (Post 1 established);

Blossoms Panel 1 Setup: Sc in each of next 4 sts, ch 1, sk next st, sc in each of next 4 sts;

Post 2 Setup: FPDC around each of next 2 sts in row below;

Interlocking Diamonds Panel Setup: Sc in each of next 3 sts, FPDC around next st in row below, sc in each of next 4 sts, FPDC around next st in row below, sc in each of next 2 sts, FPDC around next st in row below, sc in each of next 4 sts, FPDC around next st in row below, sc in each of next 3 sts;

Post 3 Setup: FPDC around each of next 2 sts in row below;

Blossoms Panel 2 Setup: Sc in each of next 4 sts, ch 1, sk next st, sc in each of next 4 sts;

Left Border: FPDC around each of next 2 sts in row below (Post 4 established), sc in next and each st to end, turn.

7 Row 4; Left Border: Ch 1 (do not count as st), sc in first st, *sl st loosely in next st, sc in next st*, rep from * to * across next 8 (10, 12, 16, 20) sts, sc in next st, sc in each of next 2 FPDC;

Blossoms 2: Sc in each sc and ch-sp to next FPDC;

Post 3: Sc in each of next 2 FPDC;

Interlocking Diamonds: Sc in next and each st to next pair of FPDC;

Post 2: Sc in each of next 2 FPDC;

Blossoms 1: Sc in each sc and ch-sp to next FPDC (Post 1);

Right Border: Sc in each of next 3 sts, *sl st loosely in next st, sc in next st*, rep from * to * across to last st, sc in last st, turn.

8 Cont even in panels and st pats as established, starting with Crumpled Seed st row 3 (see page 83); Blossoms panel row 5 (see page 81); Interlocking Diamonds panel row 5 (see page 86); and working FPDC for Posts 1, 2, 3, and 4. (See "Sweater Pattern Summary" on page 34.) At same time on every WS row maintain sc edge sts, work 1 sc in st preceding the first FPDC in Post 4. Cont until 14½ (14½, 15, 15½, 16)" from beg of ribbing, ending with WS row completed.

Armhole Shaping

9 **Next Row (RS):** Ch 1 (do not count as st), sc in first st, work in panels and st pats as established across to last 5 (5, 6, 8, 9) sts, sc in next st, turn. Rem sts unworked. [66 (70, 73, 79, 86) sts]

10 Rep last row once more. [62 (66, 68, 72, 78) sts]

11 **Next Row:** Ch 1 (do not count as st), sc2tog, sc in next st (selvage established), work in panels and st pats as established across to last 3 sts, sc in next st, sc2tog, (selvage established), turn. [60 (64, 66, 70, 76) sts]

Next Row: Ch 1 (do not count as st), sc in each of first 2 sts, work in panels and st pats as established across to last 2 sts, sc in each of last 2 sts, turn.

12 Rep step 11 (last 2 rows) 18 (19, 19, 20, 21) more times. Fasten off. [24 (26, 28, 30, 34) sts]

FRONT

1 Work as for Back to step 12 of Armhole Shaping.

2 Rep step 11 of Back 3 (4, 3, 3, 3) more times. [54 (56, 60, 64, 70) sts]

Left Shoulder Shaping

3 With RS facing, place st marker in each of 2 center sts.

Next Row (Dec Row; RS): Ch 1 (do not count as st), sc2tog, sc in next st (selvage maintained), work in panels and st pats as established across to 2 sts before first marker, sc in each of next 2 sts (selvage established), turn. Rem sts unworked. [25 (26, 28, 30, 33) sts]

4 **Next Row (Dec Row):** Ch 1 (do not count as st), sc2tog, sc in next st, work in panels and st pats as established across to last 2 sts, sc in each of last 2 sts, turn. [24 (25, 27, 29, 32) sts]

Next Row (Dec Row): Ch 1 (do not count as st), sc2tog, sc in next st, work in panels and st pats as established across to last 2 sts, sc in each of last 2 sts, turn. [23 (24, 26, 28, 31) sts]

5 Rep step 4 (last 2 rows) 9 (10, 11, 12, 13) more times. [5 (4, 4, 4, 5) sts]

6 **Next Row:** Ch 1 (do not count as st), sc in each st to end, turn.

Next Row (RS; Dec Row): Ch 1 (do not count as st), sc2tog, sc in each st to end, turn. [4 (3, 3, 3, 4) sts]

7 Rep step 6 (last 2 rows) until 1 st rem. Fasten off.

Right Shoulder Shaping

8 With RS facing, working into last full-width row and starting at inner edge of left front neck shaping, sk center 2 sts with markers.

Next Row (RS): Join yarn with sc in next st (count as st), sc in next st, work in st pats as established in previous row to last 3 sts, sc in next st, sc2tog, turn. [25 (26, 28, 30, 33) sts]

9 **Next Row (Dec Row):** Ch 1 (do not count as st), sc in each of first 2 sts, work in st pats as established across to last 3 sts, sc in next st, sc2tog, turn. [24 (25, 27, 29, 32) sts]

Next Row (Dec Row): Ch 1 (do not count as st), sc in each of first 2 sts, work in st pats as established across to last 3 sts, sc in next st, sc2tog, turn. [23 (24, 26, 28, 31) sts]

10 Rep step 9 (last 2 rows) 9 (10, 11, 12, 13) more times. [5 (4, 4, 4, 5) sts]

11 **Next Row (WS):** Ch 1 (do not count as st), sc in first st and each st to end, turn.

Next Row (Dec Row): Ch 1 (do not count as st), sc in each of first 2 sts, work in st pats as established across to last 3 sts, sc in next st, sc2tog, turn. [4 (3, 3, 3, 4) sts]

12 Rep step 11 (last 2 rows) until 1 st rem. Fasten off.

SLEEVE *(Make 2)*

1 With smaller hook, ch 10.

Foundation Row: Sc in 2nd ch from hook (count as st) and in each ch to end. [9 sc]

Ribbing

2 **Row 2:** Ch 1 (do not count as st), sc blo in first and each st to end, turn.

Single Crochet Rib st pat established.

3 Work even in st pat (rep step 2, row 2) for 29 (29, 29, 33, 33) more rows.

Sleeve Body

4 With larger hook, pivot to work across one long edge of ribbing as follows:

Row 1 (RS): Ch 1 (do not count as st), sc in end of each row, turn. [31 (31, 31, 35, 35) sc]

5 **Row 2; Border 2 Setup:** Ch 1 (do not count as st), sc in first st, *sl st **loosely** in next st, sc in next st*, rep from * to * across next 6 (6, 6, 8, 8) sts (Crumpled Seed st pat established);

Posts and Blossoms Panel Setup: Sc in each of next 13 sts;

Border 1 Setup: Sc in next st, *sl st in next st, sc in next st*, rep from * to * across to last st, sc in last st, turn.

6 **Row 3; Border 1:** Ch 1 (do not count as st), sc in first 9 (9, 9, 11, 11) sts;

Post 1 Setup: FPDC around each of next 2 sts in row below;

Blossoms: Sc in each of next 4 sts, ch 1, sk next st, sc in each of next 4 sts;

Post 2: FPDC around each of next 2 sts in row below;

Border 2: Sc in next and each st to end, turn.

7 **Row 4 (Inc Row); Border 2:** Ch 1 (do not count as st), 2 sc in first st, sc in next st, *sl st **loosely** in next st, sc in next st*, rep from * to * across to first FPDC;

Post 2: Sc in each of next 2 FPDC;

Blossoms: Sc in each sc and ch-sp to next FPDC;

Post 1: Sc in each of next 2 FPDC,

Border 1: Sc in first st, *sl st **loosely** in next st, sc in next st*, rep from * to * across to last 2 sts, sl st **loosely** in next st, 2 sc in last st, turn. [33 (33, 33, 37, 39) sts]

In the following step, start with Crumpled Seed st row 3 for Borders 1 and 2, Blossoms panel row 5, and work FPDC for Posts 1 and 2.

8 Work even in panels and st pats as established for 3 more rows.

Next Row (Inc Row): Ch 1 (do not count as st), 2 sc in next st, work in st pat as established across to last st, 2 sc in last st, turn. [35 (35, 35, 39, 41) sts]

9 Rep step 8 (last 4 rows) 11 (12, 12, 13, 14) more times. **At same time** maintain sc in first and last st of every row. [57 (59, 59, 65, 69) sts]

10 Work even in st pats as established until 16 (16½, 17, 17, 17½)" from beg, ending with WS row completed.

Raglan Shaping

11 Work as for Back Armhole Shaping. Fasten off. [11 (11, 9, 9, 9) sts]

FINISHING

1 If necessary, block all garment pieces (see page 92).

2 With smaller hook and RS facing, sc 38 (40, 40, 42, 44) sts across each raglan armhole edge on both sleeves, and armhole edges on both front and back of body, fasten off. This creates a selvage on each raglan that will make it easy to join the sleeves to the body.

3 Place one sleeve raglan edge along corresponding edge of body. With WS together, sew edges with stitches matching. (See page 92 for seaming options.) Attach rem raglan sleeve edge to body in same manner. Sew rem sleeve to body.

4 Sew back and front at side and underarm seams.

NECKBAND

1 With smaller hook, beg at top of left front neck and work as follows:

Row 1; Left Front Neck Edge: Join yarn with sc (count as st), sc 22 (24, 24, 26, 28) sts to center front, sc2tog over 2 unworked sts at center front, place marker in completed st;

Right Front Neck Edge: Work 22 (24, 24, 26, 28) sc;

Right Sleeve Top: Work 8 (8, 8, 6, 6) sc;

Back Neck: Work 18 (20, 20, 22, 24) sc;

Left Sleeve Top: Work 8 (8, 8, 6, 6) sc, turn. [80 (86, 86, 88, 94) sts]

2 **Row 2 (WS):** Ch 1 (do not count as st), sc in first and each st to 2 sts before marker, sc2tog, sc in center front stitch, move marker, sc2tog, sc in next and each st to end, turn.

3 **Row 3; Left Front Neck Edge (RS):** Ch 1 (do not count as st), sc in first st, *FPDC around next st in row below, sc in next st*, rep from * to * across to 2 sts before center front stitch;

Center Front Decrease: FPDC around next st in row below leaving last 2 lps of FPDC on hook (sk st in previous row that's behind post st), draw up lp in next st and leave on hook, YO, draw through all 3 lps on hook (dec made), FPDC around center front st, move marker (sk st in previous row that's behind post st), draw up a lp in next st and leave on hook, FPDC around next st in row below leaving last 2 lps of FPDC on hook, YO, draw yarn through all 4 lps on hook (dec made);

Right Front Neck Edge: *Sc in next st, FPDC around next st in row below*, rep from * to * to last st, sc in last st, turn.

4 Rep steps 2 and 3 (last 2 rows) once more.

5 Rep step 2 (row 2) once more.

6 **Next Row; Left Front Neck Edge:** Ch 1 (do not count as st), sc in first st, *FPDC around next st in row below, sc in next st*, rep from * to * across to 2 sts before center front stitch;

Center Front Decrease: *FPDC around next st in row below leaving last 2 lps of FPDC on hook, draw up lp in next st and leave on hook, rep from * to * once more (5 lps on hook), FPDC around next st in row below, leaving last 2 lps of FPDC on hook, YO, draw yarn through all 6 lps on hook (the last 5 sts worked together as one);

Right Front Neck Edge: *Sc in next st, FPDC around next st in row below*, rep from * to * across to last st, sc in last st. Fasten off.

7 With RS together, join collar at left shoulder.

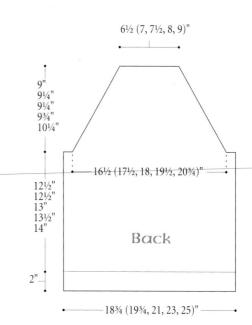

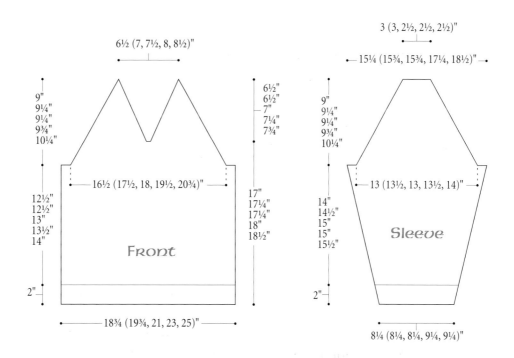

Celtic Challenge

It's time to enjoy the simple pleasures of life, like a walk in the woods while wearing a lovingly stitched sweater. A classic neutral yarn enhances the high-relief bobbles, cables, and posts.

▌ *Featured Panel and Stitch Patterns*

Plaited Cable . . . . *see page 87*
Post Rib . . . . *see "Back," "Ribbing," steps 2–3 on page 42*
Winding Road . . . . *see page 90*

▌ *Supplies*

7 (4.5 mm) crochet hook
H/8 (5 mm) crochet hook
4 stitch markers
4 buttons, ¾" (2 mm) diameter

▌ *Gauge*

13 sts and 16 rows to 4" in single crochet with H/8 (5 mm) hook

▌ *Sizing and Finished Sweater Measurements*

	EXTRA SMALL	SMALL	MEDIUM	LARGE	EXTRA LARGE
TO FIT BUST	31½"	34¼"	37¼"	41"	43¼"
FINISHED BUST	37"	41½"	44¾"	48½"	50¾"
SHOULDER LENGTH	6"	7"	7¾"	8¼"	8½"
SLEEVE LENGTH	18"	18½"	19"	19½"	20"
CENTER BACK LENGTH*	21¾"	22¼"	22¾"	23¼"	24¼"

Measurement includes neckband.

▌ *Yarn Requirements*

STYLECRAFT *SPECIALARAN* *WITH WOOL* #3005 CREAM	EXTRA SMALL	SMALL	MEDIUM	LARGE	EXTRA LARGE
	2 balls	2 balls	2 balls	3 balls	3 balls

A luxurious Plaited Cable marches up the center of each sleeve and continues across the shoulder. This "saddle" is made by continuing to work only the cable panel stitches after the desired sleeve length is reached. The sleeves, bottom, and front are all trimmed with a few rows of ribbing.

This sweater's texture is created by alternating two stitch patterns across every row. Vertical post stitches make it easier to find the beginning and end of each repeat. Since the Winding Road stitch pattern is a 16-row repeat and the Plaited Cable stitch pattern a four-row repeat, the work is somewhat challenging. Once the panels are established across the row, in subsequent rows all you have to do is make sure that you work the appropriate row of each panel. To help you sort this out, the corresponding rows are listed in the "Sweater Pattern Summary" that follows.

▮ Sweater Pattern Summary

SWEATER PANEL ROW	WINDING ROAD PANEL ROW	PLAITED CABLE PANEL ROW
6	3	3
7	4	4
8	5	5
9	6	2
10	7	3
11	8	4
12	9	5
13	10	2
14	11	3
15	12	4
16	13	5
17	14	2
18	15	3
19	16	4
20	17	5
21	18	2
22	19	3

Cont with sweater rows 7–22

BACK

1 With smaller hook, ch 59 (67, 71, 77, 81).

Foundation Row: Dc in 4th ch from hook (count as 2 sts) and in each ch to end. [57 (65, 69, 75, 79) dc]

Ribbing

2 Row 2: Ch 2 (count as hdc), FPDC around next st (2nd st from edge), *BPDC around next st, FPDC around next st*, rep from * to * across to last st, hdc in last st (top of tch), turn.

3 Row 3: Ch 2 (count as hdc), BPDC around first post st in row below, *FPDC around next post st in row below, BPDC around next post st in row below*, rep from * to * across to last st, hdc in last st (top of ch-2 tch), turn.

Body

4 Change to larger hook.

Row 4 (RS): Ch 1 (do not count as st), sc in first and each st to end, turn.

5 Row 5: Ch 1 (do not count as st), sc in first and each st to end of row, turn.

6 Row 6 (RS); Right Border: Ch 1 (do not count as st), sc in each of first 1 (5, 7, 10, 12) sts, place marker;

Plaited Cable Panel 1 Setup: FPDC around next st in row below, sc in each of next 2 sts, FPDC around each of next 4 sts in row below, sc in each of next 2 sts, FPDC around next st in row below;

Winding Road Panel 1 Setup: Sc in next st, FPDC around each of next 2 sc in row below, sc in each of next 5 sc, place marker;

Central Plaited Cable Panel Setup: FPDC around next st in row below, *sc in each of next 2 sts, FPDC around each of next 4 sts in row below, sc in each of next 2 sts, FPDC around next st in row below*, rep from * to * once more (2 st pat reps made, with 2nd rep excluding beginning post st);

Winding Road Panel 2 Setup: As Winding Road Panel 1 Setup, place marker;

Plaited Cable Panel 2 Setup: As Plaited Cable Panel 1 Setup;

Left Border: Sc in next and each st to end, turn.

Sweater pat established. Throughout back, move markers to current row as encountered.

7 **Row 7; Left Border and Plaited Cable Panel 2:** Ch 1 (do not count as st), sc in first and each st to marker;

Winding Road Panel 2: Sc in each of next 2 sc, dc in next st leaving 2 lps on hook, dc in same st leaving 3 lps on hook, dc in same st leaving 4 lps on hook, close with YO and pull through all lps on hook (bobble made, see page 75), sc in each of next 5 sc;

Central Plaited Cable Panel: Sc in next and each st to marker;

Winding Road Panel 1: As Winding Road Panel 2;

Plaited Cable Panel 1 and Right Border: Sc in next and each st to end, turn.

8 **Row 8; Right Border:** Ch 1 (count as st), sc in first and each st to marker;

Plaited Cable Panel 1: FPDC around first post st in row below, *sc in each of next 2 sts, cb4 over next 4 post sts, sc in each of next 2 sts, FPDC around next post st in row below*;

Winding Road Panel 1: Sc in each of next 2 sts, FPDC around each of next 2 FPDC in row below, sc in each of next 4 sc;

Central Plaited Cable Panel: As step 8 of Plaited Cable Panel 1 once, then from * to * of Plaited Cable Panel 1 once;

Winding Road Panel 2: As step 8 of Winding Road Panel 1;

Plaited Cable Panel 2: As step 8 of Plaited Cable Panel 1;

Left Border: Sc in next and each st to end, turn.

9 Work even in panels and borders as established to end of sweater pattern row 22 (see page 42). Beg with Winding Road panel row 6 (see page 90) and Plaited Cable panel row 2 (see page 87).

Note: Central Plaited Cable Panel combines two panels. To make a second panel, do not work the first FPDC and 2 sc in rows 3 and 5 of the Plaited Cable panel (see page 87).

10 Rep sweater rows 7–22 to cont panels and borders as established until 20 (20½, 21, 21½, 22½)" from beg. Fasten off.

RIGHT FRONT

1 With smaller hook, ch 31 (35, 37, 41, 43).

Foundation Row: Dc in 4th ch from hook (count as 2 dc) and in each ch to end. [29 (33, 35, 39, 41) dc]

Ribbing

2 **Row 2 (RS):** Ch 2 (count as hdc), FPDC around next st (2nd st from edge), *BPDC around next st, FPDC around next st *, rep from * to * across to last st, hdc in last st (top of tch), turn.

3 **Row 3:** Ch 2 (count as hdc), BPDC around first post st in row below, *FPDC around next post st in row below, BPDC around next post st in row below*, rep from * to * across to last st, hdc in last st (top of ch-2 tch), turn.

Body

4 Change to larger hook.

Row 4 (Inc Row; RS): Ch 1 (count as st), 2 (2, 2, 1, 1) sc in first st, sc in next and each st to end, turn. [30 (34, 36, 39, 41) sc]

5 **Row 5:** Ch 1 (do not count as st), sc in first and each st to end, turn.

6 **Row 6; Plaited Cable Panel 1 Setup:** Ch 1 (do not count as st), sc in first st (edge stitch established), FPDC around next st in row below, sc in each of next 2 sts, FPDC around each of next 4 sts in row below, sc in each of next 2 sts, FPDC around next st in row below;

Winding Road Panel Setup: Sc in next st, FPDC around each of next 2 sc in row below, sc in each of next 5 sc, place marker;

Plaited Cable Panel 2 Setup: FPDC around next st in row below, sc in each of next 2 sts, FPDC around each of next 4 sts in row below, sc in each of next 2 sts, FPDC around next st in row below;

Side Border: Sc in next and each st to end, turn.

Sweater pat established. Throughout front, move markers to current row as encountered.

7 **Row 7; Side Border and Plaited Cable Panel 2:** Ch 1 (do not count as st), sc in first and each st to marker;

Winding Road Panel: Sc in each of next 2 sc, bobble in next st, sc in each of next 5 sc;

Plaited Cable Panel 1: Sc in next and each st to end, turn.

8 **Row 8; Plaited Cable Panel 1:** Ch 1 (do not count as st), sc in first st, *FPDC around first post st in row below, sc in each of next 2 sts, cb4 over next 4 post sts, sc in each of next 2 sts, FPDC around next post st in row below*;

Winding Road Panel: Sc in each of first 2 sts, FPDC around each of next 2 FPDC in row below, sc in each of next 4 sc;

Plaited Cable Panel 2: Following Plaited Cable Panel 1, rep from * to * once;

Side Border: Sc in next and each st to end, turn.

Sweater st pat established.

9 Work even in panels and border as established, starting with Plaited Cable panel row 2 (see page 87) and Winding Road panel row 6 (see page 90) until 12½ (13, 13, 13, 13½)" from beg, ending with WS row completed.

Right Neck Shaping

10 **Next Row (Dec Row; RS):** Ch 1 (do not count as st), sc2tog, work in st pats as established to end, turn. [29 (33, 35, 38, 40) sc]

Next Row: Work even in panels and border as established to end, turn.

11 Rep step 10 (last 2 rows) 7 more times. [22 (26, 28, 31, 33) sc]

12 **Next Row (Dec Row):** Ch 1 (do not count as st), sc2tog, work in st pats as established to end, turn. [21 (25, 27, 30, 32) sc]

Work even in sweater pat as established for 3 rows.

13 Rep step 12 (last 4 rows) 1 (2, 2, 3, 4) more times. [20 (23, 25, 27, 28) sts]

14 Work even in panels and border as established until 20 (20½, 21, 21½, 22½)" from beg.

LEFT FRONT

1 Work as for Right Front steps 1–5.

2 **Row 6 (RS); Side Border:** Ch 1 (do not count as st), sc in first 1 (5, 7, 10, 12) sts;

Plaited Cable Panel 2 Setup: *FPDC around next st in row below, sc in each of next 2 sts, FPDC around each of next 4 sts in row below, sc in each of next 2 sts, FPDC around next st in row below*;

Winding Road Panel Setup: Sc in next st, FPDC around each of next 2 sc in row below, sc in each of next 5 sc, place marker;

Throughout left front, move markers to current row as encountered.

Plaited Cable Panel 1 Setup: As step 2 Plaited Cable Panel 2 Setup from * to *, sc in next st (edge st established), turn.

3 Row 7; Plaited Cable Panel 1: Ch 1 (do not count as st), sc in first and each st to marker;

Winding Road Panel: Sc in each of next 2 sc, bobble in next st, sc in each of next 5 sc;

Plaited Cable Panel 2 and Side Border: Sc in next and each st to end, turn.

4 Row 8; Border: Ch 1 (do not count as st), sc in first and each st to first post st;

Plaited Cable Panel 2: *FPDC around next post st in row below, sc in each of next 2 sts, cb4 over next 4 post sts, sc in each of next 2 sts, FPDC around next post st in row below*;

Winding Road Panel: Sc in each of first 2 sts, FPDC around each of next 2 FPDC in row below, sc in each of next 4 sc;

Plaited Cable Panel 1: As step 4 Plaited Cable Panel 2 from * to *, sc in next st (edge st), turn.

Sweater st pat established.

5 Work even in panels and border as established, starting with Plaited Cable panel row 2 (see page 87) and Winding Road panel row 6 (see page 90), until 12½ (13, 13, 13, 13½)" from beg, ending with WS row completed.

Left Neck Shaping

6 Next Row (Dec Row, RS): Ch 1 (do not count as st), work in panels and border as established across to last 2 sts, sc2tog, turn. [29 (33, 35, 38, 40) sc]

Next Row: Work even in panels and border as established to end, turn.

7 Rep step 6 (last 2 rows) 7 more times [22 (26, 28, 31, 33) sc]

8 Next Row (Dec Row): Ch 1 (do not count as st), work in pats as established across to last 2 sts, sc2tog, turn. [21 (25, 27, 30, 32) sc]

Work even in pat as established for 3 rows.

9 Rep step 8 (last 4 rows) 1 (2, 2, 3, 4) more times. [20 (23, 25, 27, 28) sts]

10 Work even in pat as established until 20 (20½, 21, 21½, 22½)" from beg.

SLEEVE *(Make 2)*

1 With smaller hook, ch 32.

2 Foundation Row: Dc in 4th ch from hook (count as 2 sts) and in each ch to end. [29 dc]

Ribbing

3 Row 2: Ch 2 (count as hdc), FPDC around next st (2nd st from edge), *BPDC around next st, FPDC around next st*, rep from * to * across to last st, hdc in last st (top of tch), turn.

4 Row 3: Ch 2, BPDC around next st, *FPDC around next st in row below, BPDC around next st*, rep from * to * across to last st, hdc in last st (top of ch-2 tch), turn.

Sleeve Body

5 Change to larger hook.

Row 4 (Inc Row; RS): Ch 1 (count as st), 2 sc in first st, sc in next and each st to last st, 2 sc in last st, turn. [32 sc]

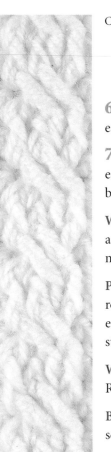

6 Row 5: Ch 1 (do not count as st), sc in first and each st to end, turn.

7 Row 6; Border 1: Ch 1 (do not count as st), sc in each of first 2 sts, FPDC around next st in row below;

Winding Road Panel 1 Setup: Sc in next st, FPDC around each of next 2 sc in row below, sc in each of next 5 sc, place marker;

Plaited Cable Panel Setup: FPDC around next st in row below, sc in each of next 2 sts, FPDC around each of next 4 sts in row below, sc in each of next 2 sts, FPDC around next st in row below;

Winding Road Panel 2 Setup: As step 7 of Winding Road Panel 1 Setup, place marker;

Border 2 Setup: FPDC around next st in row below, sc in each of last 2 sts, turn.

8 Row 7; Border 2: Ch 1 (do not count as st), sc in first and each st to marker;

Throughout sleeve, move markers to current row as encountered.

Winding Road Panel 2: Sc in next 2 sc, bobble in next st, sc in each of next 5 sc;

Plaited Cable Panel: Sc in next and each st to marker,

Winding Road Panel 1: As Winding Road Panel 2;

Border 1: FPDC around next st in row below, sc in each of last 2 sts, turn.

Sweater st pat established.

Cont in st pats as established, starting with Plaited Cable panel row 4 and Winding Road panel row 4, and shape as follows:

9 Work even as established for 3 more rows.

Next Row (Inc Row) : Ch 1 (do not count as st), 2 sc in first st, work in st pats as established across to last st, 2 sc in last st, turn. [34 sts]

10 Rep step 9 (last 4 rows) 12 (13, 14, 16, 17) more times. [58 (60, 62, 66, 68) sts]

11 Work even in st pats as established until 18 (18½, 19, 19½, 20)" from beg. Fasten off.

Saddle Shaping

12 With larger hook and WS facing, sk first 23 (24, 25, 27, 28) sts.

Next Row: Join yarn with sc in next st (count as st), work in Plaited Cable panel as established over the next 11 sts, turn. Rem sts unworked. [12 sts]

Plaited Cable is centered on Saddle.

13 Work even in st pat as established until 6 (7, 7¾, 8¼, 8½)" from beg of saddle. Fasten off.

FINISHING

1 If necessary, block all garment pieces (see page 92).

2 Sew a front shoulder to one long edge of saddle extension at top of a sleeve. Sew back shoulder to rem long edge of sleeve. Sew rem upper (unattached) edges to body armhole (see fig. 3).

3 Rep step 2 to join rem shoulder and sleeve.

4 Sew back to front at sides and sleeve underarms.

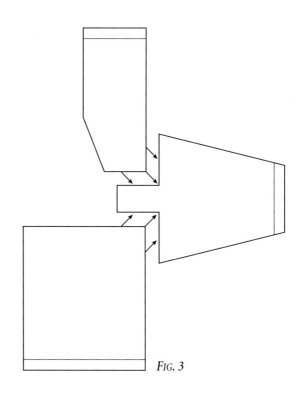

FIG. 3

BUTTON AND BUTTONHOLE BAND

1 Work with smaller hook and RS facing.

Foundation Row: Join yarn with sc in lower corner of right front (count as st), work evenly spaced sc up right front, around neckline, and down left front to lower left corner, turn. Finish with odd number of sts.

2 Row 2 (WS): Ch 3 (count as dc), dc in next and each sc to end, turn.

3 Mark buttonholes on right front with evenly spaced markers, placing first buttonhole 1" below upper corner of front and last buttonhole 1" above lower edge of bottom band.

4 Row 3: Ch 2 (count as hdc), FPDC around next st in row below, *BPDC around next st, FPDC around next st in row below *, rep from * to * across to marker, ch 1, sk 1, (buttonhole made), cont in st pat as established to end, making buttonholes at markers, turn.

5 Row 4: Ch 2 (count as hdc), BPDC around next post st in row below, *FPDC around next post st in row below, BPDC around next post st in row below*, rep from * to * across to last st, working 1 sc around each ch-sp for buttonhole, hdc in last st (top of ch-2 tch), turn. Fasten off.

6 Sew buttons to left front to correspond with buttonholes on right front.

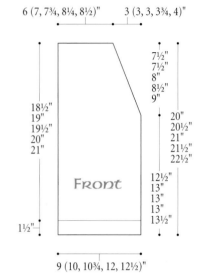

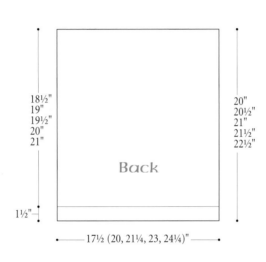

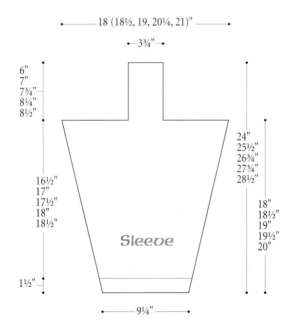

Green Mantle

A new angle on an old favorite: the classic technique for bias-stitched dishcloths is a fashion stand-out. The diagonal ridges of the bias fabric drapes softly without clinging.

Featured Stitch Pattern

Ridge .... *see "Back," step 3, on page 50*

Supplies

H/8 (5 mm) crochet hook
2 stitch markers
Knitter's pins*

Seaming is easier when pieces are first joined with large-headed, ballpoint-tip pins.

Gauge

15 sts and 13 rows to 4" in Ridge stitch pattern

Sizing and Finished Sweater Measurements

	EXTRA SMALL	SMALL	MEDIUM	LARGE	EXTRA LARGE
TO FIT BUST	31½"	34¼"	37¼"	41"	43¼"
FINISHED BUST	37"	39"	42"	46"	49"
SHOULDER LENGTH	4¾"	5¼"	6"	6½"	7¼"
SLEEVE	19"	19"	19"	19"	19"
CENTER BACK LENGTH*	25½"	26"	26"	27½"	28½"

Measurement does not include collar.

Yarn Requirements

PLYMOUTH *GALWAY HIGHLAND HEATHER* #728 GREEN GRAY	EXTRA SMALL	SMALL	MEDIUM	LARGE	EXTRA LARGE
	7 balls	8 balls	8 balls	9 balls	10 balls

This fun pattern, presented diagonally, is quite dynamic. The entire sweater is worked in two basic stitches: the half double crochet and the single crochet in the back loop only.

The bias stitching process is the same as the crocheted dishcloths that many people love to learn. Start with a few stitches and then increase at the beginning and end of every row. When the piece is the desired length, reverse the process by decreasing every row until you have the same number of stitches as the first row.

Figs. 4 and 5 show how this process is applied to "Green Mantle."

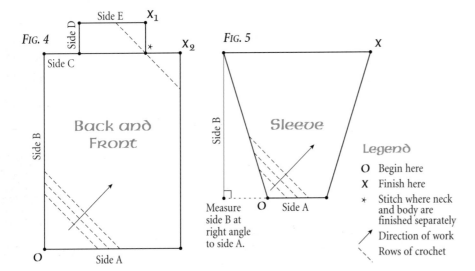

FIG. 4 — Side E, Side D, Side C, Side B, Side A, Back and Front, X₁, X₂, O

FIG. 5 — Sleeve, Side B, Side A, Measure side B at right angle to side A., O, X

Legend
O   Begin here
X   Finish here
*   Stitch where neck and body are finished separately
↗   Direction of work
╱   Rows of crochet

BACK

See fig. 4, above, to identify sides A–E.

1 Ch 2.

Foundation Row (Inc Row): Work 3 sc in 2nd ch from hook, turn. [3 sts]

2 Row 2 (Inc Row; WS): Ch 2 (count as hdc), 2 hdc in next st, 2 hdc in last st, turn. [5 sts]

3 Row 3 (Inc Row): Ch 1 (do not count as st), 2 sc in first st, sc blo in next and each st across to last st, 2 sc in last st, turn. [7 sts]

Row 4 (Inc Row): Ch 2 (do not count as st), hdc in first st (base of tch), hdc in next and each st across to last st, 2 hdc in last st, turn. [9 sts]

Ridge st pat established (hdc on WS rows, sc in blo on RS rows).

4 Rep step 3 (last 2 rows) until side A is 18½ (19½, 21, 23, 24½)" from beg, ending with RS row completed.

Side Shaping

5 Next Row (Inc Beg; Dec End; WS): Ch 2 (count as hdc), 2 hdc in next st, hdc in next and each st across to last 2 sts, hdc2tog, turn.

Next Row (Dec Beg; Inc End): Ch 1 (do not count as st), sc2tog, sc blo in next and each st across to last st, 2 sc in last st, turn.

6 Rep step 5 (last 2 rows) until side B is 25½ (26, 26, 27½ , 28½)", ending with RS row completed.

Left Shoulder Shaping

7 Next Row (Dec Row; WS): Ch 2 (count as hdc), hdc2tog, hdc in next and each st across to last 2 sts, hdc2tog, turn.

Next Row (Dec Row): Ch 1 (do not count as st), sc2tog, sc blo in next and each st across to last 2 sts, sc2tog, turn.

8 Rep step 7 (last 2 rows) until side C is 4¾ (5¼, 6, 6½, 7¼)", ending with RS row completed. Place marker.

Collar and Right Side Shaping

9 Next Row (Inc Beg; Dec End; WS): Ch 2 (count as hdc), 2 hdc in next st, hdc in next and each st across to last 2 sts, hdc2tog, turn.

Next Row (Dec Beg; Inc End): Ch 1 (do not count as st), sc2tog, sc blo in next and each st across to last st, 2 sc in last st, turn.

10 Rep step 9 (last 2 rows) until side D is 4", ending with RS row completed.

11 Next Row (Dec Row; WS): Ch 2 (count as hdc), hdc2tog, hdc in next and each st across to last 2 sts, hdc2tog, turn.

Next Row (Dec Row): Ch 1 (do not count as st), sc2tog, hdc in next and each st across to last 2 sts, sc2tog, turn.

12 Rep step 11 (last 2 rows) until side E is 9 (9, 9, 10, 10)", ending with RS row completed. Place stitch marker in current row at * on fig. 4 (see page 50). This is 9 (9, 9, 10, 10)" above stitch marker at inner edge of Side C.

Collar Finishing

13 Next Row (Dec Row; WS): Ch 2 (count as hdc), hdc2tog, hdc in next and each st across to 2 sts before stitch marker, hdc2tog, turn. Rem sts unworked.

14 Next Row (Dec Row): Ch 1 (do not count as st), sc2tog, sc blo in next and each st across to last 2 sts, sc2tog, turn.

Next Row (Dec Row): Ch 2 (count as hdc), hdc2tog, hdc in each st across to last 2 sts, hdc2tog, turn.

15 Rep step 14 (last 2 rows) until 1 st rem. Fasten off.

Right Shoulder Shaping

16 Next Row (Dec Row; WS): Join yarn with sc at marker (count as st), hdc2tog, hdc in next and each st across to last 2 sts, hdc2tog, turn.

17 Next Row (Dec Row): Ch 1 (do not count as st), sc2tog, sc blo in next and each st across to last 2 sts, sc2tog, turn.

Next Row (Dec Row): Ch 2 (count as st), hdc2tog, hdc in next and each st across to last 2 sts, hdc2tog, turn.

18 Rep step 17 (last 2 rows) until 1 st rem. Fasten off.

FRONT

Work as for Back.

SLEEVE *(Make 2)*

See fig. 5 on page 50 to identify sides A and B.

1 Ch 2.

2 Foundation Row (Inc Row; RS): 3 sc in 2nd ch from hook. [3 sts]

3 Ch 5 **loosely**, turn.

Row 2 (Inc Row): Hdc in 3rd ch from hook (count as 2 hdc) and in each of next 2 ch, hdc in next and each st across to last st, 2 hdc in last st, turn. [8 sts]

Row 3 (Inc Row): Ch 1 (do not count as st), 2 sc in first st, sc blo in next and each st across to last st, 2 sc in last st, turn. [10 sts]

4 Rep step 3 until side A is 8", ending with RS row completed. Do not turn at end of last row.

5 Ch 5, turn.

Next Row (Inc Row; WS): Hdc in 3rd ch from hook (count as 2 sts) and in each of next 2 ch, hdc in next and each st to end, turn.

Next Row (Dec Beg; Inc End): Ch 1 (do not count as st), sc2tog, sc blo in first and each st across to last st, 2 sc in last st, do not turn.

6 Rep step 5 until side B is 19", ending with RS row completed and turning at end of last row.

Note: Measure side B at a right angle to side A. Do not measure along the sloped edge of the sleeve. (See fig. 5, page 50.)

7 Next Row (Dec Row; WS): Ch 2 (count as hdc), hdc2tog, hdc in next and each st to end, turn.

Next Row (Dec Row): Ch 1 (do not count as st), sc2tog, sc blo in next and each st across to last 2 sts, sc2tog, turn.

8 Rep step 7 (last 2 rows) until 1 st rem. Fasten off.

FINISHING

1 If necessary, block all garment pieces (see page 92).

2 With knitters pins, join back to front at shoulders and collar. Diagonal ridges won't match at edges. Sew garment as pinned. (See page 92 for seaming options.)

3 On front, place stitch marker at each side (vertical edge) 10" below shoulder seam. Rep for back. Sew sleeves to body.

4 Sew side and underarm seams.

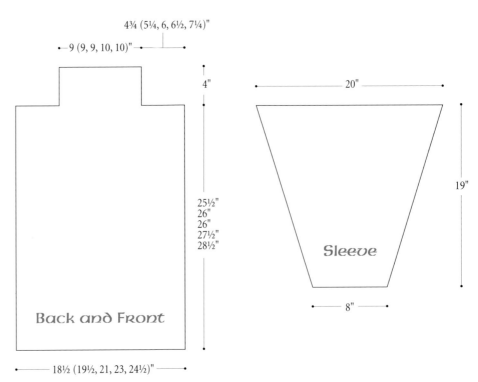

Forever Diamonds

Warm, roomy, and easy to wear, this traditionally patterned pullover is a great way to learn traveling and crossed post stitches. This sweater is sure to be your new best friend.

▌Featured Stitch Patterns

Cabled Lattice . . . . *see page 82*
Mock Post Rib . . . . *see "Cuff," steps 2–3, on page 56*

▌Supplies

7 (4.5 mm) crochet hook
H/8 (5 mm) crochet hook
2 stitch markers

▌Gauge

12 sts and 15 rows to 4" in Cabled Lattice stitch pattern with H/8 (5 mm) hook

▌Sizing and Finished Sweater Measurements

	EXTRA SMALL	SMALL	MEDIUM	LARGE	EXTRA LARGE
TO FIT BUST	31½"	34¼"	37¼"	41"	43¼"
FINISHED BUST	37"	40"	44"	47"	49"
SHOULDER LENGTH	5½"	6"	7"	7½"	7¾"
SLEEVE LENGTH	18½"	19"	19½"	19½"	20"
CENTER BACK LENGTH	26"	26½"	27"	28"	29"

▌Yarn Requirements

	EXTRA SMALL	SMALL	MEDIUM	LARGE	EXTRA LARGE
PATONS *DECOR* #1612 RICH AQUA	9 balls	10 balls	10 balls	11 balls	12 balls

BACK

1 With larger hook, ch 57 (61, 67, 71, 75).

Foundation Row: Sc in 2nd ch from hook (count as st) and in each ch to end, turn. [56 (60, 66, 70, 74) sts]

2 Row 2 (WS): Ch 1 (do not count as st), sc in each of first 0 (2, 1, 3, 1) sts, place marker, sc in each of next 56 (56, 64, 64, 72) sts, place marker for end st pat reps, sc in each of last 0 (2, 1, 3, 1) sts, turn.

3 Row 3: Ch 1 (do not count as st), sc in first and each st to marker, move marker, sc in each of next 2 sts, FPDC around next sc in row below (3rd st from edge), sc in each of next 2 sts, FPDC around next st in row below (3rd st from last FPDC), sc in each of next 4 sts, *FPDC around next sc in row below, sc in each of next 2 sts, FPDC around next st in row below, sc in each of next 4 sts*, rep from * to * across to last 6 sts, FPDC around next sc in row below (6th st from left edge), sc in each of next 2 sts, FPDC around next sc in row below (3rd st from last FPDC), sc in next 2 sts, move marker, sc in next and each st to end, turn. Cabled Lattice st pat established between markers.

4 Cont in st pat as established (starting with row 4 of Cabled Lattice st pat; see page 82), working border sts outside markers in sc and moving markers to current row to track beg and end of st pat, until 23 (23½, 24, 25, 26)" from beg. Fasten off.

FRONT

1 Work as for Back until 20¼ (20¾, 21, 22, 22¾)" from beg, ending with WS row completed.

Left Neck Shaping

2 Next Row (Dec Row; RS): Ch 1 (do not count as st), work in pat as established across first 23 (24, 27, 28, 29) sts, sc in next st, turn. Rem sts unworked.

Note: Make incomplete pat rep by working pat as established across available sts, sc in last st. Maintain 1 sc at beg and end of every row.

3 Next Row (Dec Row): Ch 1 (do not count as st), sc2tog, work in pat as established (sc in each st) to end of row, turn. [23 (24, 27, 28, 29) sts]

This pattern is a simple eight-stitch repeat. The shaping is minimal. The cuffs, waistband, and collar, all worked in a pattern that imitates the look of a knitted rib, are made with the front post double crochet and single crochet stitches. The bottom band and cuffs are added after the main pieces are finished, thus allowing you to lengthen or shorten the body and sleeves for a perfect fit.

4 Next Row (Dec Row): Ch 1 (do not count as st), work in pat as established across to last 2 sts, sc2tog, turn. [22 (23, 26, 27, 28) sts]

5 Rep steps 3–4 (last 2 rows) 2 more times. [18 (19, 22, 23, 24) sts]

6 Rep step 3 once. [17 (18, 21, 22, 23) sts]

Work even in st pat as established until 23 (23½, 24, 25, 26)" from beg. Fasten off.

Right Neck Shaping

7 With RS facing, working into last full-width row and starting at inner edge of left front neck shaping, sk next 8 (10, 10, 12, 14) sts. Working in pat as established on last full-width row, cont as follows:

Next Row (Dec Row; RS): Join yarn with sc (count as 1 st) in next st, cont in st pat as established to end, turn. [24 (25, 28, 29, 30) sts]

8 Next Row (Dec Row; WS): Ch 1 (do not count as st), work in pat as established across to last 2 sts of row, sc2tog, turn. [23 (24, 27, 28, 29) sts]

9 Next Row (Dec Row): Ch 1 (do not count as st), sc2tog, work in pat as established to end, turn. [22 (23, 26, 27, 28) sts]

10 Rep steps 8–9 (last 2 rows) 2 more times. [18 (19, 22, 23, 24) sts]

11 Rep step 8 once more. [17 (18, 21, 22, 23) sts]

Work even until 23 (23½, 24, 25, 26)" from beg. Fasten off.

SLEEVE *(Make 2)*

1 With larger hook, ch 33.

Foundation Row: Sc in 2nd ch from hook (count as 1 st) and in each ch to end, turn. [32 sts]

2 Row 2 (WS): Ch 1 (do not count as st), sc in first and each st to end, turn.

3 Row 3: Ch 1 (do not count as st), sc in each of first 2 sts, FPDC around next sc in row below (3rd st from edge), sc in each of next 2 sts, FPDC around next st in row below (3rd st from last FPDC), sc in each of next 4 sts, *FPDC around next sc in row below, sc in each of next 2 sts, FPDC around next st in row below, sc in each of next 4 sts*, rep from * to * across to last 6 sts, FPDC around next sc in row below (6th st from left edge), sc in each of next 2 sts, FPDC around next sc in row below (3rd st from last FPDC), sc in last 2 sts, turn. Cabled Lattice st pat established.

4 Row 4 (Inc Row): Ch 1 (do not count as st), 2 sc in first st, sc in next and each st to last st, 2 sc in last st, turn. [34 sts]

5 Work even in st pat as established (starting with row 5 of Cabled Lattice st pat; see page 82) for 3 rows. Cont pat as partial rep at both edges when possible, with 1 sc at beg and end of each row.

Next Row (Inc Row): As step 4. [36 sts]

6 Cont in st pat as established, rep step 5 (last 4 rows) 11 (11, 12, 12, 13) more times, working partial rep at both edges and maintaining 1 sc at beg and end of each row. [58 (58, 60, 60, 62) sts]

7 Work even in st pat as established until 15½ (16, 16½, 16½, 17)" from beg. Fasten off.

CUFF

1 With smaller hook and RS facing, work across narrowest edge of sleeve as follows:

Foundation Row: Join yarn with sc in first ch (count as st), sc in next and each ch to end. [32 sc]

2 Row 2 (WS): Ch 1 (do not count as st), sc in next and each st to end, turn.

3 Row 3 (RS): Ch 1 (do not count as st), sc in first st, *FPDC around next sc in row below, sc in next st*, rep from * to * to end, turn.

Mock Post Rib st pat established.

4 Row 4: Ch 1 (do not count as st), sc in first and each st to end, turn.

Row 5: Ch 1 (do not count as st), sc in first st, *FPDC around FPDC in row below, sc in next st*, rep from * to * to end, turn.

5 Rep step 4 (last 2 rows).

6 Work even in st pat as established (rep step 4) until 3" from beg of cuff. Fasten off.

BOTTOM BANDS

1 With smaller hook and RS facing, work across lower edge of back as follows on next page:

Foundation Row: Join yarn with sc in first ch (count as st), sc in next and each ch of base ch to end. [56 (60, 66, 70, 74) sc]

2 As steps 2–6 of Cuff. Fasten off.

3 Make bottom band for Front in same manner.

COLLAR

1 Sew back to front at right shoulder.

2 Place marker on back 7½ (8, 8, 8½, 9)" from inner edge of right shoulder seam.

3 With smaller hook and RS facing, join yarn at inner edge of left front shoulder with sc at marker (count as st), sc around neck edge to stitch marker on back, turn. Remove markers.

4 As steps 2–6 of Cuff. Fasten off.

FINISHING

1 If necessary, block all garment pieces.

2 Sew back to front at left shoulder and collar edges.

3 Sew underarm seam on each sleeve and sew sleeves into body.

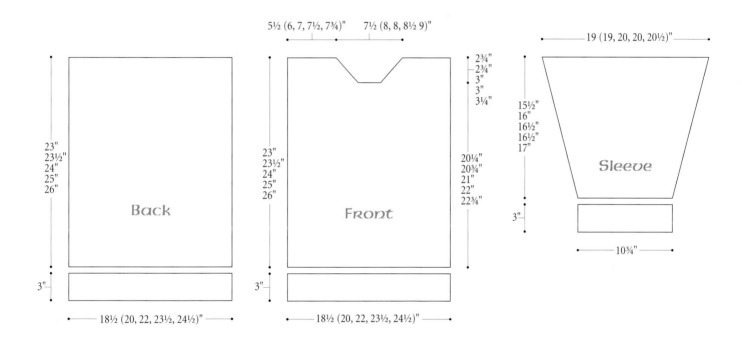

Scottish Reel

Celebrate glorious Aran stitching! A medley of

texture and patterns dance across the front, back,

and sleeves of this stitch-pattern sampler.

▌ *Featured Panel and Stitch Patterns*

▌ *Supplies*

7 (4.5 mm) crochet hook
H/8 (5 mm) crochet hook
2 stitch markers

▌ *Gauge*

14 sts and 16 rows to 4" in all st pats except Mock Cable with H/8 (5 mm) hook
14 sts and 18 rows to 4" in Mock Cable with H/8 (5 mm) hook

▌ *Sizing and Finished Sweater Measurements*

	EXTRA SMALL	SMALL	MEDIUM	LARGE	EXTRA LARGE
TO FIT BUST	31½"	34¼"	37¼"	41"	43¼"
FINISHED BUST	36"	38"	41"	44"	47"
SHOULDER LENGTH	5"	5½"	6"	6½"	7"
SLEEVE LENGTH	18"	19"	19"	19"	20"
CENTER BACK LENGTH	23"	23¾"	24½"	26"	27½"

▌ *Yarn Requirements*

PLYMOUTH *ENCORE* #9401 MEDIUM GREEN	EXTRA SMALL	SMALL	MEDIUM	LARGE	EXTRA LARGE
	8 balls	8 balls	9 balls	10 balls	11 balls

Pattern Information

We're making this easy for you! Rather than working entire garment shapes, you stitch panels, which are then assembled into garment pieces. Each vertical panel works one stitch pattern at a time, and then a cable border is worked along one edge (see figs. 6 and 7). There is simple shaping on some of the panels.

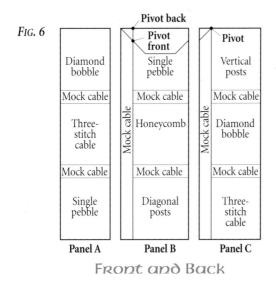

FIG. 6

Panel A — Diamond bobble / Mock cable / Three-stitch cable / Mock cable / Single pebble

Panel B — Pivot back / Pivot front / Single pebble / Mock cable / Honeycomb / Mock cable / Diagonal posts / Mock cable

Panel C — Pivot / Vertical posts / Mock cable / Diamond bobble / Mock cable / Three-stitch cable / Mock cable

Front and Back

FIG. 7

Panel G — Mock cable

Panel D — Vertical posts / Mock cable / Single pebble / Mock cable

Panel E — Pivot / Honeycomb / Mock cable / Diamond bobble / Mock cable

Panel F — Pivot / Vertical posts / Mock cable / Single pebble

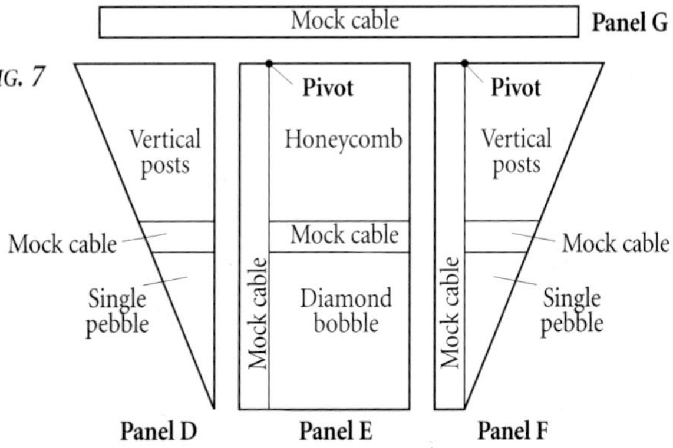

Sleeve

BACK PANEL A

1 With larger hook, ch 18 (20, 22, 24, 26).

Foundation Row: Sc in 2nd ch from hook (count as st) and each ch to end, turn. [17 (19, 21, 23, 25) sts]

Single Pebble Block

2 Row 2 (WS): Ch 1 (do not count as st), sc in first st, *hdc in next st, sl st **loosely** in next st*, rep from * to * across to last 2 sts, hdc in next st, sc in last st, turn.

Row 3: Ch 1 (do not count as st), sc in first and each st to end, turn.

Single Pebble st pat established.

3 Work even in st pat as established (rep step 2) until 6 (6¼, 6½, 7, 7½)" from beg of block, ending with WS row completed.

Mock Cable Band

4 Next Row (RS): Ch 1 (do not count as st), sc in first and each st to end, turn.

5 Next Row: Ch 1 (do not count as st), sl st **loosely** in first and each st to end, turn.

6 Rep step 4.

7 Next Row: Ch 1 (do not count as st), sc in first st, *hdc in next st, sl st in next st*, rep from * to * across to last 2 sts, hdc in next st, sc in last st, turn.

8 Rep step 4.

9 Next Row: Ch 1 (do not count as st), sl st **loosely** in first st and each st to end, turn.

10 Rep step 4.

Three-Stitch Cable Block

11 Next Row (WS): Ch 1 (do not count as st), sc in first 1 (2, 1, 2, 0) sts, place marker, sc in next 15 (15, 20, 20, 25) sts, place marker, sc in last 1 (2, 0, 1, 0) sts, turn. Move markers every row.

12 Next Row: Ch 1 (do not count as st), sc in first and each st to marker, *sc in next st, FPDC around each of next 3 sc in row below, sc in next st*, rep from * to * across to marker, sc in next and each st to end, turn.

13 Next Row: Ch 1 (do not count as st), sc in first and each st to end, turn.

Next Row: Ch 1 (do not count as st), sc in next and each st to marker, *sc in next st, cb3, sc in next st*, rep from * to * across to next marker, sc in next and each st to end, turn.

Next Row: Ch 1 (do not count as st), sc in first and each st to end, turn.

Next Row: Ch 1 (do not count as st), sc in next and each st to marker, *sc in next st, FPDC around each of next 3 post sts (2 FPDC and next FPTR) in row below, sc in next st,* rep from * to * across to marker, sc in next and each st to end, turn.

Three-Stitch Cable pat established.

14 Rep step 13 (last 4 rows) until 6 (6¼, 6½, 7, 7½)" from beg of Three-Stitch Cable Block, ending with WS row completed. Remove markers.

Mock Cable Band

15 Rep Back Panel A steps 4–10 (see page 60).

Diamond Bobble Block

16 Next Row (WS): Ch 1 (do not count as st), sc in first and each st to end, turn.

17 Rep step 16 (last row) 0 (0, 0, 2, 2) more times.

18 Next Row: Ch 1 (do not count as st), sc in each of first 2 (3, 4, 5, 6) sts, place marker, sc in each of next 13 sts, place marker, sc in next and each st to end, turn. Move markers every row.

19 Next Row: Ch 1 (do not count as st), sc in next and each st to marker, sc in each of first 6 sts, dc in next st leaving 2 lps on hook, dc in same st leaving 3 lps on hook, dc in same st leaving 4 lps on hook, close with YO and pull through all lps on hook (bobble made), sc in each of next 6 sts to marker, sc in next and each st to end, turn.

20 Work even in sc border sts and st pat as established between markers (starting with row 4, see page 84) until one motif completed. Remove markers.

21 Rep step 16 (work even in single crochet rows) until 20½ (21¼, 22, 23½, 25)" from beg. Fasten off.

BACK PANEL B

1 With larger hook, ch 18 (20, 22, 24, 26).

Foundation Row: Sc in 2nd ch from hook (count as st) and each ch to end, turn. [17 (19, 21, 23, 25) sts]

Diagonal Posts Block

2 Row 2 (WS): Ch 1 (do not count as st), sc in first 1 (1, 0, 1, 1) st, place marker, sc in each of next 15 (18, 21, 21, 24) sts, place marker, sc in next and each st to end of row, turn.

Note: In some sizes, marker for beg and/or end of row is on edge st. Move markers every row.

3 Row 3: Ch 1 (do not count as st), sc in first and each st to marker, *sc in each of next 2 sts, FPDC around next sc in row below (3rd st from last FPDC)*, rep from * to * across to next marker, sc in next and each st to end, turn.

Diagonal Posts st pat established.

4 Cont even in sc border sts and st pat as established between markers (starting with row 4, see page 83), until 6 (6¼, 6½, 7, 7½)" from beg, ending with WS row completed. Remove markers.

Mock Cable Band

5 Work as for Back Panel A steps 4–10 (see page 60).

Honeycomb Block

6 **Next Row (WS):** Ch 1 (do not count as st), sc in first 2 (3, 1, 2, 3) sts, place marker, sc in each of first 2 sts, *ch 1, sk next st, sc in each of next 2 sts*, rep from * to * 4 (4, 6, 6, 6) more times, place marker, sc in next and each st to end, turn.

Note: End-of-row marker for medium goes on last st in row.

Honeycomb st pat established between markers with sc border sts outside markers.

7 Work even in sc border sts and st pat as established between markers (starting with row 3, see page 85) until 13¼ (13¾, 14¼, 15¼, 16¼)" from beg, ending with WS row completed.

Mock Cable Band

8 Work as for Back Panel A steps 4–10 (see page 60).

Single Pebble Block

9 Work as for Back Panel A step 2 (see page 60) until work from beg of panel is 20½ (21¼, 22, 23½, 25)", ending with RS row completed.

Mock Cable Border

10 **Next Row (RS):** Pivot with RS facing, work long edge of Panel B to bottom corner as follows:

Upper Block: Ch 1 (do not count as st), work 21 (22, 23, 25, 26) sc;

Mock Cable Band: Work 5 sc;

Middle Block: Work 20 (22, 23, 24, 26) sc;

Mock Cable Band: Work 5 sc;

Lower Block: Work 20 (21, 23, 24, 27) sc, turn. [71 (75, 79, 83, 89) sts]

11 **Next Rows:** Work as for Back Panel A steps 5–10 (Mock Cable Band). Fasten off.

BACK PANEL C

1 With larger hook, ch 18 (20, 22, 24, 26).

Foundation Row: Sc in 2nd ch from hook (count as st) and each ch to end, turn. [17 (19, 21, 23, 25) sts]

Three-Stitch Cable Block

2 Work as for Back Panel A steps 11–14.

Mock Cable Band

3 Work as for Back Panel A steps 4–10.

Diamond Bobble Block

4 Work as for Back Panel A steps 16–20.

5 Work even in sc for 0 (2, 2, 4, 6) rows.

Mock Cable Band

6 Work as for Back Panel A steps 4–10.

Vertical Posts Block

7 **Next Row (WS):** Ch 1 (do not count as st), sc in first 1 (1, 0, 1, 1) st, place marker, sc in each of next 15 (18, 21, 21, 24) sts, place marker, sc in next and each st to end of row, turn. Move markers every row.

8 **Next Row:** Ch 1 (do not count as st), sc in first and each st to marker, *sc in each of next 2 sts, FPDC around next sc in row below*, rep from * to * across to marker, sc in next and each st to end, turn.

9 **Next Row:** Ch 1 (do not count as st), sc in first and each st to end, turn.

10 Next Row: Ch 1 (do not count as st), sc in first and each st to marker, *sc in each of next 2 sts, FPDC around next FPDC in row below*, rep from * to * across to marker, sc in next and each st to end, turn.

Vertical Posts st pat established.

11 Work even in sc border sts and st pat as established (rep steps 9–10) until 20½ (21¼, 22, 23½, 25)" from beg, ending with RS row completed. Remove marker.

Mock Cable Border

12 Work as for Back Panel B steps 10–11.

FRONT PANEL A

Work as for Back Panel A.

FRONT PANEL B

1 Work as for Back Panel B (steps 1–8, with step 9 partially completed) until 18 (18½, 19, 20¼, 21½)" from beg, ending with WS row completed.

Left Neck Shaping

2 Next Row (Dec Row; RS): Ch 1 (do not count as st), work in Single Pebble st pat as established in first 3 (4, 5, 6, 7) sts, turn. Rem sts unworked. [3 (4, 5, 6, 7) sts]

3 Next Row (Dec Row): Ch 1 (do not count as st), sc2tog, work in pat as established to end, turn. [2 (3, 4, 5, 6) sts]

Next Row (Dec Row): Ch 1 (do not count as st), work in pat as established across to last 2 sts, sc2tog, turn. [1 (2, 3, 4, 5) sts]

4 Rep step 3 (last 2 rows) until 1 st rem. Fasten off.

Right Neck Shaping

5 With RS facing, working into last full-width row and starting at inner edge of left neck shaping, sk next 11 sts.

Next Row: Join yarn with sc in next st (count as st), work in Single Pebble st pat as established in previous row to end, turn. [3 (4, 5, 6, 7) sts]

6 Next Row (Dec Row): Ch 1 (do not count as st), work in st pat as established across to last 2 sts, sc2tog, turn. [2 (3, 4, 5, 6) sts]

Next Row (Dec Row): Ch 1 (do not count as st), sc2tog, work in st pat as established to end, turn. [1 (2, 3, 4, 5) sts]

7 Rep step 6 (last 2 rows) until 1 st rem.

Mock Cable Border

8 Next Row (RS): Pivot with RS facing, work evenly spaced sc along long edge of Panel B to bottom corner as follows:

Upper Block: Ch 1 (do not count as st), work 15 (16, 17, 19, 20) sc;

Mock Cable Band: Work 5 sc;

Middle Block: Work 20 (22, 23, 24, 26) sc;

Mock Cable Band: Work 5 sc;

Lower Block: Work 20 (21, 23, 24, 27) sc, turn. [65 (69, 73, 77, 83) sts]

9 Row 2 (Inc Row): Ch 1 (do not count as st), sl st loosely in first and each st to last st, 2 sc in last st, turn. [68 (72, 74, 80, 84) sts]

10 Row 3 (Inc Row): Ch 1 (do not count as st), 2 sc in first st, sc in next and each st to end, turn. [69 (73, 75, 81, 85) sts]

11 Row 4 (Inc Row): Ch 1 (do not count as st), sc in first st, *hdc in next st, sl st in next st*, rep from * to * across to last 2 sts, hdc in next st, 2 sc in last st, turn. [70 (74, 76, 82, 86) sts]

12 Row 5: Ch 1 (do not count as st), 2 sc in first st, sc in next and each st to end, turn. [71 (75, 77, 83, 87) sts]

13 Row 6 (Inc row): Ch 1 (do not count as st), sl st loosely in first and each st to last st, 2 sc in last st, turn. [72 (76, 78, 84, 88) sts]

14 Row 7 (Inc Row): Ch 1 (do not count as st), 2 sc in first st, sc in next and each st to end, turn. Fasten off. [73 (77, 79, 85, 89) sts]

FRONT PANEL C

1 Work as for Back Panel C to Mock Cable Border.

Mock Cable Border

2 Next Row (RS): Pivot with RS facing and work evenly spaced sc along long edge of Panel B to bottom corner as follows:

Upper Block: Ch 1 (do not count as st), work 21 (22, 23, 25, 26) sc;

Mock Cable Band: Work 5 sc;.

Middle Block: Work 20 (22, 23, 24, 26) sc;

Mock Cable Band: Work 5 sc;

Lower Block: Work 20 (21, 23, 24, 27) sc, turn. [71 (75, 79, 83, 89) sts]

3 Next Row: Ch 1 (do not count as st), sl st loosely in first st and each st to last 2 sts, sc2tog, turn. [70 (74, 78, 82, 88) sts]

4 Next Row: Ch 1 (do not count as st), sc2tog, sc in next and each st to end, turn. [68 (72, 76, 80, 86) sts]

5 Next Row: Work in pat as established across to last 2 sts, sc2tog, turn. [67 (71, 75, 79, 85) sts]

Next Row: Ch 1 (do not count as st), sc2tog, work in pat as established to end, turn. [66 (70, 74, 78, 84) sts]

6 Rep step 5 (last 2 rows) once. Fasten off. [65 (69, 73, 77, 83) sts]

BACK PANELS ASSEMBLY

1 With larger hook and RS of Back Panel A facing, join yarn with sc in bottom right corner (count as st) and work along right edge of panel as follows:

Lower Block: Work 20 (21, 23, 24, 26) sc;

Mock Cable Band: Work 5 sc;

Middle Block: Work 20 (21, 23, 24, 26) sc;

Mock Cable Band: Work 5 sc;

Upper Block: Work 20 (21, 23, 24, 26) sc. Fasten off. [70 (73, 79, 82, 88) sts]

2 With Back Panel B, rep step 1.

3 With WS together, sew right (single crochet) edge of Back Panel A to Mock Cable Border edge of Back Panel B, matching top and bottom corners of each block. With every crocheted edge stitch matched, sew joined pieces.

4 Follow step 3 to join Back Panel B to Back Panel C.

FRONT PANELS ASSEMBLY

1 Rep "Back Panels Assembly" steps 1–3 to join Front Panels A and B.

2 Rep "Back Panels Assembly" step 1 to edge stitch Front Panel B, except make only 15 (16, 17, 19, 20) sc along edge of upper block. [65 (68, 73, 77, 82) sts]

3 Rep "Back Panels Assembly" step 3 to join Front Panels B and C.

BACK BOTTOM BAND

1 With smaller hook and RS facing, work along bottom of joined back panels as follows:

Foundation Row: Join yarn with a sc (count as st) in bottom corner, work evenly spaced sc to opposite corner, turn. Finish with odd number of sts.

2 Rep Back Panel A steps 5–10 (Mock Cable Band).

3 Rep Back Panel A steps 5–10 (Mock Cable Band).

4 Rep Back Panel A steps 5–9. Fasten off.

FRONT BOTTOM BAND

As Back Bottom Band.

SLEEVE PANEL D (Make 2)

1 With larger hook, ch 2.

Foundation Row: Work 2 sc in 2nd ch from hook (count as st), turn. [2 sts]

2 Row 2 (Inc Row; WS): Ch 1 (do not count as st), 2 sc in first st, sc in next st, turn. [3 sts]

Single Pebble Block

3 Work as for Back Panel A Single Pebble block **except** inc 1 st at beg of every WS row 12 times, ending with WS row completed. [15 sts]

4 Cont in st pat as established, inc 1 st at beg of every 4th (WS) row until 6½ (7, 7, 7, 7½)" from beg, ending with WS row completed.

Mock Cable Band

5 Rep Back Panel A steps 4–10, **at same time** cont inc 1 st at beg of every 4th row.

Vertical Posts Block

6 Work as for Back Panel C steps 7–10, **at same time** cont inc at beg of every 4th row to 23 sts, then cont in Vertical Posts st pat as established (rep Back Panel C steps 9–10), until 14¼ (15¼, 15¼, 15¼, 16¼)" from beg. Fasten off.

SLEEVE PANEL E (Make 2)

1 With larger hook, ch 18.

Foundation Row: Sc in 2nd ch from hook (count as st) and each ch to end, turn. [17 sts]

2 **Row 2 (RS):** Ch 1 (do not count as st), sc in next and each st to end, turn.

3 Rep step 2 (row 2) 0 (2, 2, 2, 2) more times.

Diamond Bobble Block

4 Work as for Back Panel A steps 18–20.

5 Work even in sc for 2 (2, 2, 2, 4) rows.

Mock Cable Band

6 Work as for Back Panel A steps 4–10.

Honeycomb Block

7 **Next Row (WS):** Ch 1 (do not count as st), sc in first 2 (3, 1, 2, 3) sts, place marker, sc in each of first 2 sts, *ch 1, sk next st, sc in each of next 2 sts*, rep from * to * 4 more times, place marker, sc in next and each st to end, turn.

Honeycomb st pat established.

8 Work even in sc border sts and st pat as established between markers (starting with row 3, see page 84), until 14¼ (15¼, 15¼, 15¼, 16¼)" from beg, ending with RS row completed.

Mock Cable Border

9 **Next Row (RS):** Pivot with RS facing, work evenly spaced sc along vertical edge of Panel E to bottom corner as follows:

Upper Block: Ch 1 (do not count as st), work 23 (24, 24, 24, 26) sc;

Mock Cable Band: Work 5 sc;

Lower Block: Work 23 (24, 24, 24, 26) sc, turn. [51 (53, 53, 53, 57) sts]

10 **Next Rows:** Work as for Back Panel A steps 5–10. Fasten off.

SLEEVE PANEL F (Make 2)

1 With larger hook, ch 2.

Foundation Row: Work 2 sc in 2nd ch from hook (count as st), turn. [2 sts]

2 **Row 2 (Inc Row; WS):** Ch 1 (do not count as st), 2 sc in first st, sc in next st, turn. [3 sts]

Mock Cable Band

5 Rep Back Panel A steps 4–10, **at same time** cont inc 1 st at end of every 4th row.

Vertical Posts Block

6 Work as for Back Panel C steps 7–10, **at same time** cont inc at end of every 4th row to 23 sts, then cont in Vertical Posts st pat as established (rep Back Panel C steps 9–10) until 14¼ (15¼, 15¼, 15¼, 16¼)" from beg, ending with RS row completed.

Mock Cable Border

7 Next Row (RS): Pivot with RS facing, work evenly spaced sc along vertical edge of Panel F to bottom corner as follows:

Upper Block: Ch 1 (do not count as st), work 23 (24, 24, 24, 26) sc;

Mock Cable Band: Work 5 sc;

Lower Block: Work 23 (24, 24, 24, 26) sc, turn. [51 (53, 53, 53, 57) sts]

8 Next Rows: Work as for Back Panel A steps 5–10 (Mock Cable Band). Fasten off.

SLEEVE PANELS ASSEMBLY

1 With larger hook and RS of Sleeve Panel D facing, join yarn with sc in bottom right corner (count as st) and work along right edge of panel as follows:

Lower Block: Work 23 (24, 24, 24, 26) sc;

Mock Cable Band: Work 5 sc;

Upper Block: Work 23 (24, 24, 24, 26) sc. Fasten off. [51 (53, 53, 53, 57) sts]

2 Rep step 1 with Sleeve Panel E.

3 With WS together, sew right (single crochet) edge of Sleeve Panel D to Mock Cable Border edge of Sleeve Panel E, matching top and bottom corners of each block. With every crocheted edge stitch matched, sew joined pieces. In the same manner, join Sleeve Panel E to Sleeve Panel F.

Single Pebble Block

3 Work as for Back Panel A Single Pebble Block **except** inc 1 st at end every WS row 12 times, ending with WS row completed. [15 sts]

4 Cont in st pat as established, inc 1 st at end of every 4th (WS) row until 6½ (7, 7, 7, 7½)" from beg, ending with WS row completed.

SLEEVE PANEL G

1 With larger hook and RS facing, work across top:

Foundation Row: Join yarn with sc (count as st) in top right corner, work evenly spaced sc to opposite corner. Finish with odd number of sts.

2 Rep Back Panel A steps 5–10. Fasten off.

CUFF

With smaller hook and RS facing, work across bottom of sleeve as for Back Bottom Band.

NECKBAND

1 Sew back to front at right shoulder seam.

2 Place marker on back and another on front at inner edge of left shoulder 5 (5½, 6, 6½, 7)" from edge.

3 With smaller hook and RS facing, work as follows:

Foundation Row: Join yarn with sc (count as st) at marker on front, work evenly spaced sc around neck edge to marker on back, turn.

4 Work as for Back Panel A steps 4–10. Fasten off.

FINISHING

1 Sew back to front at left shoulder and neckband.

2 Sew sleeves to joined front and back and then join body at sides and sleeve underarms. (See page 92 for seaming options.)

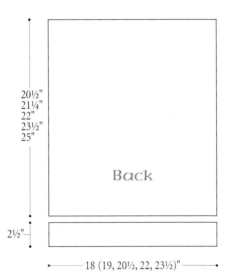

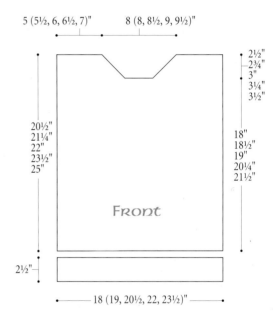

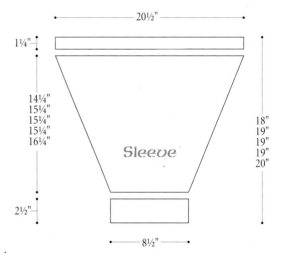

Summer Solstice

As the days get shorter, chase away the chill with a richly textured cotton sweater. The look is complex, but the work is simple.

Featured Stitch Patterns

Mock Cable . . . . *see page 87*
Single Weave . . . . *see page 88*

Supplies

7 (4.5 mm) crochet hook
H/8 (5 mm) crochet hook
Stitch marker

Gauge

14 sts and 20 rows to 4" in Single Weave with H/8 (5 mm) hook
14 sts and 18 rows to 4" in Mock Cable with H/8 (5 mm) hook

Sizing and Finished Sweater Measurements

	EXTRA SMALL	SMALL	MEDIUM	LARGE	EXTRA LARGE
TO FIT BUST	31½"	34¼"	37¼"	41"	43¼"
FINISHED BUST	32½"	36"	39½"	43"	45"
SHOULDER LENGTH	3"	3¾"	4½"	5"	5½"
SLEEVE LENGTH	18½"	19"	19"	20"	20"
CENTER BACK LENGTH	18"	18½"	19"	19½"	20"

Yarn Requirements

	EXTRA SMALL	SMALL	MEDIUM	LARGE	EXTRA LARGE
CASCADE *SIERRA* #03 IVORY	7 balls	7 balls	8 balls	8 balls	9 balls

Pattern Information

Whatever your skill level, this is a great sweater for you to try. All you need to know are the slip, single, and half double crochet stitches. Then use the spike single crochet to create the delicate look of the Single Weave pattern. As figs. 8, 9, and 10 show, the lower portion of the back, front, and sleeves are the Single Weave stitch pattern (see page 88). Then the work switches to the Mock Cable stitch pattern (see page 87) for the upper portion. After some assembly, the bottom band, cuffs, and collar are worked with a few rows of the Mock Cable border.

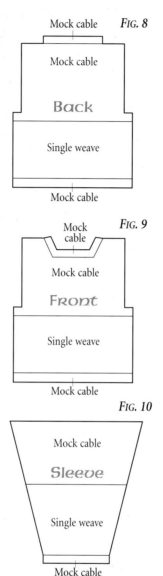

FIG. 8

Mock cable

Mock cable

Back

Single weave

Mock cable

FIG. 9

Mock cable

Mock cable

Front

Single weave

Mock cable

FIG. 10

Mock cable

Sleeve

Single weave

Mock cable

BACK

1 With larger hook, ch 58 (64, 70, 76, 80).

Foundation Row: Sc in 2nd ch from hook (count as st) and each ch to end, turn. [57 (63, 69, 75, 79) sts]

2 **Row 2 (RS):** Ch 1 (do not count as st), sc in first st, *ch 1, sk next st, sc in next st*, rep from * to * to end, turn.

3 **Row 3:** Ch 1 (do not count as st), sc in first st, *sc in skipped st in row below by working around previous row (ssc made; see page 74), ch 1, sk next sc*, rep from * to * across to last 2 sts, ssc in next sc in row below, sc in last st, turn.

4 **Row 4:** Ch 1 (do not count as st), sc in first st, *ch 1, sk next ssc, ssc in next (skipped) sc in row below*, rep from * to * across to last 2 sts, ch 1, sk next ssc, sc in last st, turn.

Row 5: Ch 1 (do not count as st), sc in first st, *ssc in next (skipped) ssc in row below, ch 1, sk next ssc*, rep from * to * across to last 2 sts, ssc in next ssc in row below, sc in last st, turn.

Single Weave st pat established.

5 Work even in st pat as established (rep step 4, last 2 rows) until 7½ (7½, 8, 8, 8)" from beg, ending with WS row completed.

Stitch Pattern Change

6 **Next Row (Single Weave Finishing Row; RS):** Ch 1 (do not count as st), sc in each of first 2 sts, *ssc in next (skipped) ssc in row below, sc in next ssc in previous row*, rep from * to * across to last st, sc in last st, turn.

7 **Next Row:** Ch 1 (do not count as st), sl st **loosely** in first and each st to end, turn.

8 **Next Row:** Ch 1 (do not count as st), sc in first and each st to end, turn.

9 **Next Row:** Ch 1 (do not count as st), sc in first st, *hdc in next st, sl st in next st*, rep from * to * across to last 2 sts, hdc in next st, sc in last st, turn.

Mock Cable st pat established.

10 Rep step 8.

11 Rep step 7.

Armhole Shaping

12 **Next Row (Dec Row):** Ch 1 (do not count as st), sc in first and each st to last 4 sts, turn. Rem sts unworked. [53 (59, 65, 71, 75) sts]

13 Rep step 12 (last row). [49 (55, 61, 67, 71) sts]

14 Work even in st pat as established (starting with row 2, see page 87) until 17 (17½, 18, 18½, 19)" from beg. Fasten off.

70

FRONT

1 Work as for Back, including armhole shaping, until 14½ (14¾, 15¼, 15½, 16)" from beg, ending with WS row completed.

Left Neck Shaping

2 Next Row (Dec Row; RS): Work in Mock Cable st pat as established (sc in each st) across next 19 (21, 24, 26, 27) sts, turn. Rem sts unworked.

3 Next Row (Dec Row): Ch 1 (do not count as st), sc2tog, work in pat as established to end, turn. [18 (20, 23, 25, 26) sts]

4 Next Row (Dec Row): Ch 1 (do not count as st), work in pat as established (sc in each st) to last 2 sts, sc2tog, turn. [17 (19, 22, 24, 25) sts]

5 Rep steps 3–4 (last 2 rows) 3 more times. [11 (13, 16, 18, 19) sts]

6 Rep step 3 once. [10 (12, 15, 17, 18) sts]

7 Work even in st pat as established until 17 (17½, 18, 18½, 19)" from beg. Fasten off.

Right Neck Shaping

8 With RS facing, working into last full-width row and starting at inner edge of left front neck shaping, sk next 11 (13, 13, 15, 17) sts.

Next Row (RS): Join yarn with sc in next st (count as st), work in Mock Cable st pat as established on last full-width row (sc in each st) across rem sts. [19 (21, 24, 26, 27) sts]

9 Next Row (Dec Row): Ch 1 (do not count as st), work in st pat as established across to last 2 sts, sc2tog, turn. [18 (20, 23, 25, 26 sts]

10 Next Row (Dec Row): Ch 1 (do not count as st), sc2tog, work in st pat as established to end, turn. [17 (19, 22, 24, 25) sts]

11 Rep steps 9–10 (last 2 rows) 3 more times. [11 (13, 16, 18, 19) sts]

12 Rep step 9 once more. [10 (12, 15, 17, 18) sts]

13 Work even until 17 (17½, 18, 18½, 19)" from beg. Fasten off.

SLEEVE *(Make 2)*

1 With larger hook, ch 32.

Foundation Row: Sc in 2nd ch from hook (count as st) and in each ch to end, turn. [31 sts]

2 Row 2 (RS): Ch 1 (do not count as st), sc in first st, *ch 1, sk next st, sc in next st*, rep from * to * to end, turn.

3 Row 3: Ch 1 (do not count as st), sc in first st, *sc in skipped st in row below by working around previous row (ssc made, see page 74), ch 1, sk next sc*, rep from * to * across to last 2 sts, ssc in next sc in row below, sc in last st, turn.

4 Row 4 (Inc Row): Ch 1 (do not count as st), 2 sc in first st, *ch 1, sk next ssc, ssc in next skipped st in row below*, rep from * to * across to last 2 sts, ch 1, sk next ssc, 2 sc in last st, turn. [33 sts]

5 Row 5: Ch 1 (do not count as st), sc in first st, ch 1, sk next st, *ssc in next (skipped) ssc in row below, ch 1, sk next ssc*, rep from * to * across to last st, sc in last st, turn.

Single Weave st pat established.

Cont even in st pat as established for 2 more rows.

Next Row (Inc Row): Ch 1 (do not count as st), 2 sc in next st, work in pat as established across to last st, 2 sc in last st, turn. [35 sts]

6 Rep step 5 (last 4 rows) until 10" from beg, ending with WS row completed.

7 As Back steps 6–11 (Stitch Pattern Change and Mock Cable st pat), **at same time** cont inc at beg and end of every 4th row to 63 (65, 65, 67, 67) sts and cont st pat as established. On row following each inc row, maintain sc edge sts but work rem sts in Mock Cable st pat as established.

8 Work even in st pats as established until 17½ (18, 18, 19, 19)" from beg. Fasten off.

CUFF

1 Work with smaller hook and RS of sleeve facing.

Foundation Row: Join yarn with sc in corner (count as st), sc in next and each st of base ch to end, turn. [31 sc]

2 Row 2 (WS): Ch 1 (do not count as st), sl st **loosely** in first and each st to end, turn.

3 Row 3: Ch 1 (do not count as st), sc in first and each st to end, turn.

4 Row 4: Ch 1 (do not count as st), sc in first st, *hdc in next st, sl st in next st*, rep from * to * across to last 2 sts, hdc in next st, sc in last st, turn.

5 Row 5: As step 3 (row 3).

6 Row 6: As step 2 (row 2). Fasten off.

COLLAR

1 If necessary, block all garment pieces (see page 92).

2 Sew back to front at right shoulder. (See page 92 for seaming options.)

3 Place marker on back 8 (8¼, 8½, 9, 9¼)" from shoulder seam.

4 Work with smaller hook and RS facing.

Foundation Row: Join yarn with sc in last row at top corner of left front neck. Work evenly spaced sc around neck edge to left back neck marker, turn. Finish with odd number of sts.

5 As steps 2–6 of Cuff. Fasten off.

BOTTOM BAND

1 Sew back to front at both sides. (See page 92 for seaming options.)

2 Work with smaller hook and RS facing.

Foundation Row: Join yarn with sc at bottom of left side seam (count as st), sc in each ch of base chain around lower edge of front and back, returning to left side seam, turn. Do not work rem pat in rounds.

3 As steps 2–6 of Cuff. Fasten off.

FINISHING

1 Sew back to front at left shoulder and collar. (See page 92 for seaming options.)

2 Sew together bottom band edges.

3 Sew underarm seam on each sleeve and sew sleeves into body.

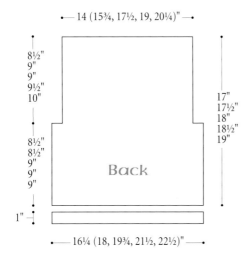

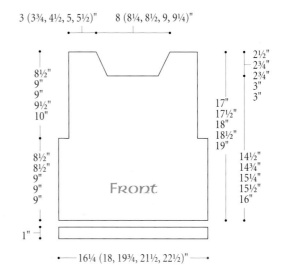

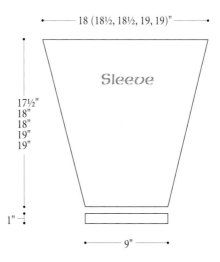

Featured Stitches Guide

Ready for some fun? You're going to love transforming the most basic crochet stitches (slip, chain, single, double, treble) into exciting new shapes. This isn't going to take you long, because you only need to learn 10 stitches in order to make every sweater in this book. The following step-by-step instructions and illustrations will walk you through every stitch that's new to you. If you're stumped by any of the abbreviations used in these instructions, you can look them up on page 91.

SSC

SPIKE SINGLE CROCHET

This is a dramatic stitch that's created by drawing a loop through a lower row and then completing a stitch in the usual manner. Two rows must be completed before starting a row that includes a spike stitch.

1 Insert the hook into the next (usually skipped) stitch in the row below, from front to back (fig. 11).

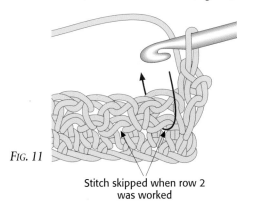

FIG. 11

Stitch skipped when row 2
was worked

2 Wrap the yarn over the hook, draw a loop through to the front of the work and up to the same height as the current row (fig. 12).

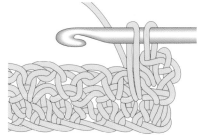

FIG. 12

3 Wrap the yarn over the hook and pull it through both loops on the hook (fig. 13).

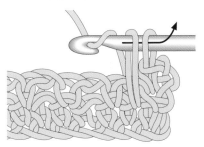

FIG. 13

74

rsc

REVERSE SINGLE CROCHET

The humble single crochet stitch becomes a delicate corded edging when worked from left to right, along the right side of the work.

1 Working in the opposite direction and swinging the hook down and under your hand, insert the hook, from front to back, in the next stitch to the right (fig. 14).

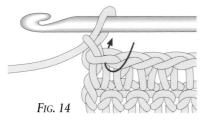

FIG. 14

2 Wrap the yarn over the hook and draw a loop through to the front of the work (fig. 15).

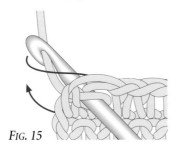

FIG. 15

3 Wrap the yarn over the hook and draw it through both loops on the hook (fig. 16).

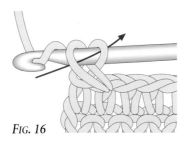

FIG. 16

bobble

BOBBLE

Worked from the wrong side, the finished bobble is a cluster of stitches that looks like a puffball on the right side of the crocheted fabric.

1 Start a double crochet stitch in the usual manner: Wrap the yarn over the hook, insert the hook from front to back in the next stitch, wrap the yarn over the hook, pull the loop to the front of the work, wrap the yarn over the hook, pull a loop through the first two loops on the hook (fig. 17).

Note: Single crochet edge stitch in figs. 17, 18, and 19 are not part of the bobble.

FIG. 17

2 Start another double crochet stitch in the usual manner: Wrap the yarn over the hook, insert the hook in the same stitch in the current row from front to back, wrap the yarn over the hook, pull the loop to the front of the work, wrap the yarn over the hook, pull the loop through the first two loops on the hook (fig. 18).

FIG. 18

3 Repeat step 2 once more (making one more incomplete double crochet stitch), so that there are four loops remaining on the hook.

4 Wrap the yarn over the hook and pull the loop through all the loops on the hook (fig. 19).

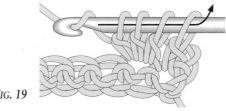

FIG. 19

BPDC

BACK POST DOUBLE CROCHET

This is little more than a double crochet stitch that's worked into the row below rather than the previous row. The post of the finished stitch is recessed from the surface. The illustrations for this stitch show a single crochet edge stitch because post stitches shouldn't be worked at an edge.

1 Wrap the yarn over the hook. From the back of the work, insert the hook between the current and next stitch (between the first and second stitches if working into the second stitch) in the row below. Now bring the hook to the back of the work by inserting it, from front to back, on the opposite side of the next stitch in the row below (fig. 20).

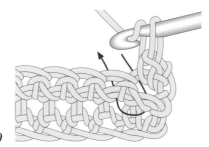

FIG. 20

2 Wrap the yarn over the hook, draw a loop to the front, then to the back of the work.

3 Wrap the yarn over the hook and pull it through two loops on the hook (fig. 21).

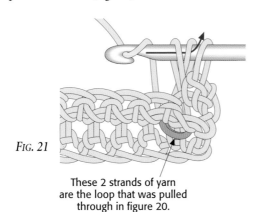

FIG. 21

These 2 strands of yarn are the loop that was pulled through in figure 20.

4 Rep step 3 once.

Note 1: A post stitch counts as one stitch in the current row. To work even, skip the stitch in the previous row that's in front or behind the post stitch (fig. 22).

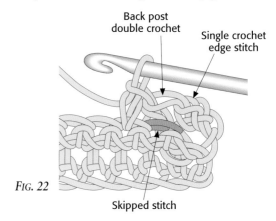

Back post double crochet

Single crochet edge stitch

FIG. 22

Skipped stitch

Note 2: In later rows, you may need to work a back or front post double crochet around a post stitch in the row below. To do this, insert the hook around the post rather than through the upper loops of the stitch. Fig. 23 shows a front post double crochet stitch being worked around a back post double crochet stitch made in the previous row.

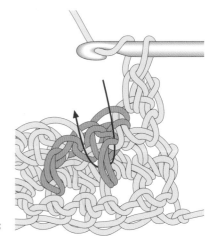

FIG. 23

FPDC and FPTR

FRONT POST DOUBLE AND TREBLE CROCHETS

Both the front post double crochet and the front post treble crochet are little more than the basic stitches worked into an earlier row. Because it's worked on the front of the fabric, the finished post stitch is raised from the surface. The illustrations for both of these stitches start with a single crochet edge stitch because post stitches shouldn't be worked at an edge.

Note that the post stitch begins by inserting the hook between the first and second stitches (fig. 24). This placement is crucial for accurate stitching across a row. The following steps, plus figs. 24 and 25, explain the front post double crochet. Fig. 26 shows a front post treble crochet.

1 Wrap the yarn over the hook. From the front of the work, insert the hook between the current and next stitches in the row below, on the right side of the specified stitch. Now bring the hook to the front of the work by inserting it, from back to front, on the other side of the next stitch in the row below (fig. 24).

2 Wrap the yarn over the hook and then draw a loop to the back, then to the front of the work.

3 Wrap the yarn over the hook and pull a loop through two of the loops on the hook.

4 Rep step 3 once (fig. 25).

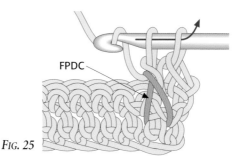

FPDC

FIG. 25

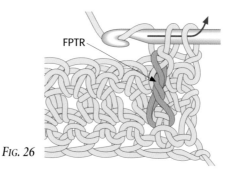

FPTR

FIG. 26

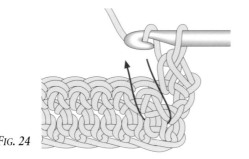

FIG. 24

cb2

TWO-STITCH CABLE

This cable is made over two adjacent stitches in the row below.

1 Skip the next double crochet (or front post double crochet) stitch in the row below.

2 Work a front post double crochet stitch around the next double crochet (or front post double crochet) stitch in the row below (fig. 27).

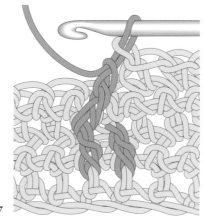

FIG. 27

3 Working in front of the front post double crochet stitch just made, make a front post double crochet stitch around the skipped double crochet (or front post double crochet) stitch in the row below (fig. 28).

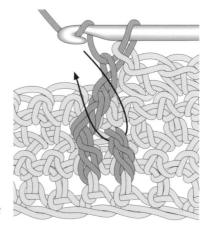

FIG. 28

Note: To complete the row as directed, start the next stitch in the third available stitch in the current row. In other words, do not work into the two stitches in the previous row, which are behind the two front post double crochet stitches just made.

cb3

THREE-STITCH CABLE

This stitch creates a cable over three post stitches in the row below.

1 Skip the first double crochet (or front post double crochet) stitch in the row below.

2 Work a front post double crochet stitch around the post of the second double crochet (or front post double crochet) stitch in the row below.

3 Work another front post double crochet stitch around the post of the third double crochet (or front post double crochet) stitch in the row below (fig. 29).

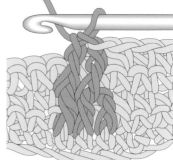

FIG. 29

4 Working in front of the two stitches just made, work a front post treble crochet stitch around the first (skipped) double crochet (or front post double crochet) stitch in the row below (fig. 30).

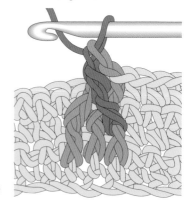

FIG. 30

Note: To complete the row as directed, start the next stitch in the fourth available stitch in the current row. In other words, do not work into the three stitches behind the front post double and treble crochet stitches just made.

<table>
<tr><td>cb4</td><td></td><td>TWL</td></tr>
</table>

FOUR-STITCH CABLE

This cable is made over four adjacent post stitches.

1 Skip the first two stitches in the row below.

2 Work a front post treble crochet stitch around the post of the third front post double crochet stitch in the row below (fig. 31).

3 Work a front post treble crochet stitch around the post of the fourth front post double crochet stitch in the row below (fig. 31).

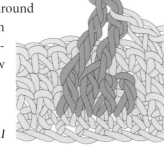

FIG. 31

4 Work a front post treble crochet stitch around the first front post double crochet stitch in the row below (fig. 32).

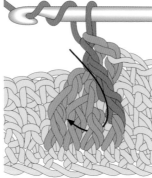

FIG. 32

5 Work a front post treble crochet stitch around the second front post double crochet stitch in the row below (fig. 33).

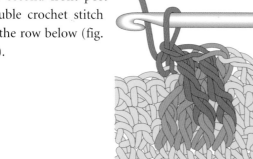

FIG. 33

Note: Do not work into the four stitches behind the four front post treble crochet stitches just made (fig. 33).

TWIST LEFT

The following steps move a post stitch diagonally to the left by one stitch position.

1 Make a single crochet stitch in the next stitch (fig. 34).

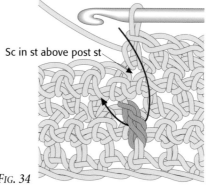

Sc in st above post st

FIG. 34

2 In the row below, there's a post stitch (FPDC or FPTR) that corresponds with the position of the single crochet stitch worked in step 1. Work a front post double crochet stitch around it (fig. 35).

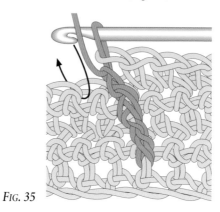

FIG. 35

Note: A front post double crochet stitch counts as one stitch in the current row. To work even, skip the stitch in the previous row that's behind this post stitch. When a TWL is followed immediately by a TWR (twist right), you end up skipping two stitches in the previous row (see fig. 38 on page 80).

TWR

TWIST RIGHT

This moves a post stitch diagonally to the right.

1 Make a front post double crochet stitch around the closest post stitch (FPDC or FPTR) in the row below (fig. 36).

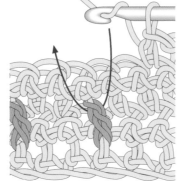

FIG. 36

2 Skip the next stitch. Single crochet in the next stitch (fig. 37).

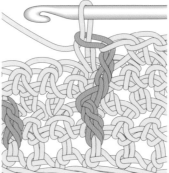

FIG. 37

Note: A twist right can be worked after a twist left, over four stitches. Single crochet stitches are in positions 1 and 4, with two front post double crochet stitches in the center. The two center stitches in the previous row, which are behind the post stitches, are unworked (fig. 38).

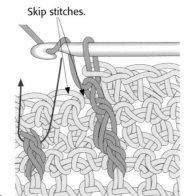

Skip stitches.

FIG. 38

cr2

POST STITCH CROSS

Built on front post and single crochet stitches.

1 Skip the first front post double crochet stitch in the row below.

2 Work a front post treble crochet stitch around the next (second) front post double crochet in the row below (fig. 39.)

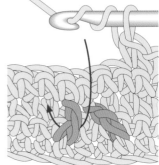

FIG. 39

3 Skip the stitch in the previous row that's behind the front post treble crochet stitch.

4 Make a single crochet stitch in each of the next two stitches (fig. 40).

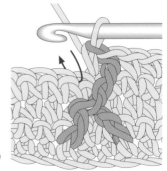

FIG. 40

5 Working in front of the front post treble crochet stitch just made, work a front post treble crochet stitch around the first (skipped) front post double crochet stitch in the row below (fig. 41).

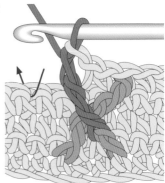

FIG. 41

Note: To complete the cr2, skip the stitch in the previous row (behind the most recent post stitch) and make the next stitch specified.

Pattern Work Encyclopedia

A simple mixture of basic stitches can create a beautiful landscape of textures. You can learn a large number of new crochet patterns by using traditional stitches in innovative ways. Now you can create some beautiful crocheted fabric using the stitches that you learned in the "Featured Stitches Guide" on pages 74–80. Some of the panels and patterns will help you stretch your skills, while others need little more than a few basic stitches.

BLOSSOMS PANEL

Worked in Cottage Wear
(see page 32)
Worked over 9 sts
(add 1 ch for base ch)

▌ *Featured Stitches*

Bobble . . . . *see page 75*
Chain (ch)
Chain-space (ch-sp)
Front post double crochet (FPDC). . *see page 77*
Single crochet (sc)
Treble (tr)

▌ *Instructions*

Foundation Row: Sc in 2nd ch from hook and each ch to end, turn.

Row 2 (WS): Ch 1 (do not count as st), sc in first and each st to end, turn.

Row 3: Ch 1 (do not count as st), sc in each of first 4 sts, ch 1, sk next st, sc in each of last 4 sts, turn.

Row 4: Ch 1 (do not count as st), sc in each of first 4 sts, sc around ch-sp, sc in each of last 4 sts, turn.

Row 5: Ch 1 (do not count as st), sc in each of first 2 sts, *tr in skipped sc in row 2, sc in next st, dc in same skipped sc in row 2, sc in next st, tr in same skipped sc in row 2, sc in each of last 2 sts, turn.

Row 6: Ch 1 (do not count as st), sc in first st, *dc in next st leaving 2 lps on hook, dc in same st leaving 3 lps on hook, dc in same st leaving 4 lps on hook, close with YO and pull through all lps on hook (bobble made, see page 75), sc in each of next 4 sts, bobble in next st, sc in each of last 2 sts, turn.

Row 7: Ch 1 (do not count as st), sc in each of first 4 sts, FPDC around dc in row 5, sc in each of last 4 sts, turn.

Row 8: Ch 1 (do not count as st), sc in each of first 4 sts, bobble in next st, sc in each of last 4 sts, turn.

Row 9: Ch 1 (do not count as st), sc in first and each of next 8 sts, turn.

Row 10: Ch 1 (do not count as st), sc in first and each of next 8 sts, turn.

Rows 2–10 form Blossoms panel rep.

CABLED LATTICE STITCH PATTERN

Worked in Forever Diamonds
(see page 53)

Multiple of 8 sts + 8 sts
(also add 1 ch for base ch)

▌ *Featured Stitches*

Chain (ch)
Front post double crochet (FPDC). . *see page 77*
Front post treble crochet (FPTR). . . *see page 77*
Post stitch cross (cr2) . . . . *see page 80*
Single crochet (sc)
Twist left (TWL). . . . . *see page 79*
Twist right (TWR). . . . . *see page 80*

▌ *Instructions*

Foundation Row: Sc in 2nd ch from hook (count as 1 st) and in each ch to end, turn.

Row 2 (WS): Ch 1 (do not count as st), sc in first and each st to end, turn.

Row 3: Ch 1 (do not count as st), sc in each of first 2 sts, FPDC around next sc in row below (3rd st from edge), sc in each of next 2 sts, FPDC around next st in row below (3rd st from last FPDC), sc in each of next 4 sts, *FPDC around next sc in row below (5th st from last FPDC), sc in each of next 2 sts, FPDC around next st in row below (3rd st from last FPDC), sc in each of next 4 sts*, rep from * to * across to last 6 sts, FPDC around next sc in row below (6th st from left edge), sc in each of next 2 sts, FPDC around next sc in row below (3rd st from last FPDC), sc in last 2 sts, turn.

Row 4 and All WS Rows: Ch 1 (do not count as st), sc in first and each st to end, turn.

Row 5: Ch 1 (do not count as st), sc in first 2 sts, *TWL over next 2 sts, TWR over next 2 sts, sc in each of next 4 sts*, rep from * to * across to last 6 sts, TWL over next 2 sts, TWR over next 2 sts, sc in each of next 2 sts, turn.

Row 7: Ch 1 (do not count as st), sc in first 2 sts, *cr2 over next 4 sts, sc in each of next 4 sts*, rep from * to * across to last 6 sts, cr2 over next 4 sts, sc in each of next 2 sts, turn.

Row 9: Ch 1 (do not count as st), sc in first st, *TWR over next 2 sts, sc in each of next 2 sts, TWL over next 2 sts, sc in each of next 2 sts*, rep from * to * across to last 7 sts, TWR over next 2 sts, sc in each of next 2 sts, TWL over next 2 sts, sc in last st, turn.

Row 11: Ch 1 (do not count as st), sc in each of first 2 sts (ignore first post st in row below), *sc in each of next 4 sts, TWL over next 2 sts, TWR over next 2 sts*, rep from * to * across to last 6 sts, sc in each of last 6 sts, turn.

Row 13: Ch 1 (do not count as st), sc in each of first 2 sts, *sc in each of next 4 sts, cr2 over next 4 sts*, rep from * to * across to last 6 sts, sc in each of last 6 sts, turn.

Row 15: Ch 1 (do not count as st), sc in each of first 2 sts, *sc in each of next 4 sts, FPDC around FPTR in row below, sc in each of next 2 sts, FPDC around FPTR in row below*, rep from * to * across to last 6 sts, sc in each of last 6 sts, turn.

Row 17: Ch 1 (do not count as st), sc in each of first 2 sts, *sc in each of next 4 sts, TWL over next 2 sts, TWR over next 2 sts*, rep from * to * across to last 6 sts, sc in each of last 6 sts, turn.

Row 19: Ch 1 (do not count as st), sc in each of first 2 sts, *sc in each of next 4 sts, cr2 over next 4 sts*, rep from * to * across to last 6 sts, sc in each of last 6 sts, turn.

Row 21: Ch 1 (do not count as st), sc in each of first 2 sts, FPDC around next st in row below (3rd st from edge), *sc in each of next 2 sts, TWR over next 2 sts, sc in each of next 2 sts, TWL over next 2 sts*, rep from * to * across to last 5 sts, sc in each of next 2 sts, FPDC around next st in row below (4th st from left edge), sc in each of last 2 sts, turn.

Row 23: Ch 1 (do not count as st), sc in each of first 2 sts, *TWL over next 2 sts, TWR over next 2 sts, sc in each of next 4 sts*, rep from * to * across to last 6 sts, TWL over next 2 sts, TWR over next 2 sts, sc in each of next 2 sts, turn.

Row 25: Ch 1 (do not count as st), sc in each of first 2 sts, *cr2 over next 4 sts, sc in each of next 4 sts*, rep from * to * across to last 6 sts, cr2 over next 4 sts, sc in each of next 2 sts, turn.

Row 27: Ch 1 (do not count as st), sc in each of first 2 sts, *FPDC around FPTR in row below, sc in each of next 2 sts, FPDC around FPTR in row below, sc in each of next 4 sts*, rep from * to * across to last 6 sts, FPDC around FPTR in row below, sc in each of next 2 sts, FPDC around FPTR in row below, sc in last 2 sts, turn.

Rows 4–27 form Cabled Lattice st pat rep.

CRUMPLED SEED STITCH PATTERN

Worked in Rugged Rover, Ivy League, and Cottage Wear
(see pages 14, 26, and 32)
Multiple of 2 sts + 1 st
(also add 1 ch for base ch)

▌ *Featured Stitches*

Chain (ch)
Single crochet (sc)
Slip stitch (sl st)

▌ *Instructions*

Foundation Row: Sc in 2nd ch from hook (count as st) and each ch to end, turn.

Row 2 (WS): Ch 1 (do not count as st), sc in first st, *sl st **loosely** in next st, sc in next st*, rep from * to * to end, turn.

Row 3 (RS): Ch 1 (do not count as st), sc in first and each st to end, turn.

Rows 2–3 form Crumpled Seed st pat rep.

DIAGONAL POSTS STITCH PATTERN

Worked in Scottish Reel
(see page 58)
Multiple of 3 sts + 3 sts
(also add 1 ch for base ch)

▌ *Featured Stitches*

Chain (ch)
Front post double crochet (FPDC) .. *see page 77*
Single crochet (sc)
Twist left (TWL) . . . . *see page 79*

▌ *Instructions*

Foundation Row: Sc in 2nd ch from hook (count as st) and each ch to end, turn.

Row 2 (WS): Ch 1 (do not count as st), sc in each st to end, turn.

Row 3: Ch 1 (do not count as st), sc in first st, FPDC around next sc in row below (2nd st from edge), *sc in each of next 2 sts, FPDC around next sc in row below (3rd st from last FPDC)*, rep from * to * across to last st, sc in last st, turn.

Rows 4, 6, and 8 (WS): Ch 1 (do not count as st), sc in first and each st to end, turn.

Row 5: Ch 1 (do not count as st), sc in first st, *TWL over next 2 sts, sc in next st*, rep from * to * across to last 2 sts, sc in each of last 2 sts, turn.

Row 7: Ch 1 (do not count as st), sc in each of first 2 sts, *TWL over next 2 sts, sc in next st*, rep from * to * across to last st, sc in last st, turn.

Row 9: Ch 1 (do not count as st), sc in first st, FPDC around next sc in row below (2nd st from edge), *sc in next st, TWL over next 2 sts*, rep from * to * across to last st, sc in last st, turn.

Rows 4–9 form Diagonal Posts st pat rep.

DIAMOND BOBBLE PANEL

Worked in Scottish Reel
(see page 58)
Worked over 13 sts
(add 1 ch for base ch)

▌ *Featured Stitches*

Bobble . . . . *see page 75*
Chain (ch)
Double crochet (dc)
Single crochet (sc)

▌ *Instructions*

Foundation Row: Sc in 2nd ch from hook (count as st) and each ch to end, turn.

Row 2: Ch 1 (do not count as st), sc in first and each st to end, turn.

Row 3 (WS): Ch 1 (do not count as st), sc in each of first 6 sts, dc in next st leaving 2 lps on hook, dc in same st leaving 3 lps on hook, dc in same st leaving 4 lps on hook, close with YO and pull through all lps on hook (bobble made, see page 75), sc in each of next 6 sts, turn.

Row 4 and All RS Rows: Ch 1 (do not count as st), sc in first and each st to end, turn.

Row 5: Ch 1 (do not count as st), sc in each of first 5 sts, bobble in next st, sc in next st, bobble in next st, sc in each of next 5 sts, turn.

Row 7: Ch 1 (do not count as st), sc in each of first 4 sts, bobble in next st, sc in each of next 3 sts, bobble in next st, sc in each of next 4 sts, turn.

Row 9: Ch 1 (do not count as st), sc in each of first 3 sts, bobble in next st, sc in each of next 5 sts, bobble in next st, sc in each of next 3 sts, turn.

Row 11: Ch 1 (do not count as st), sc in each of first 2 sts, bobble in next st, sc in each of next 3 sts, bobble in next st, sc in each of next 3 sts, bobble in next st, sc in each of next 2 sts, turn.

Row 13: Ch 1 (do not count as st), sc in first st, bobble in next st, sc in each of next 3 sts, bobble in next st, sc in next st, bobble in next st, sc in each of next 3 sts, bobble in next st, sc in last st, turn.

Row 15: Rep row 11.

Row 17: Rep row 9.

Row 19: Rep row 7.

Row 21: Rep row 5.

Row 23: Rep row 3.

Rows 2–23 form Diamond Bobble panel rep.

DOUBLE POSTS AND RIDGES STITCH PATTERN

Worked in Morning Mist
(see page 8)
Multiple of 7 sts + 7 sts
(also add 1 ch for base ch)

▌ *Featured Stitches*

Chain (ch)
Front post double crochet (FPDC) . . *see page 77*
Single crochet (sc)
Single crochet in back loop only (sc blo)

▌ *Instructions*

Foundation Row: Sc in 2nd ch from hook (count as 1 st) and in each ch to end, turn.

Row 2 (WS): Ch 1 (do not count as st), sc in first and each st to end, turn.

Row 3: Ch 1 (do not count as st), sc blo in each of first 2 sts, FPDC around each of next 2 sts in row below (3rd and 4th sts from edge), sc blo in each of next 5 sts, *FPDC around each of next 2 sts in row below, sc blo in each of next 5 sts*, rep from * to * across to last 5 sts, FPDC around each of next 2 sts in row below (6th and 7th sts from last FPDC), sc blo in each of the next 3 sts, turn.

Row 4: Ch 1 (do not count as st), sc in first and each st to end, turn.

Row 5: Ch 1 (do not count as st), sc blo in each of first 2 sts, *FPDC around each of next 2 FPDC in row below, sc blo in each of next 5 sts*, rep from * to * across to last 5 sts, FPDC around each of next 2 FPDC in row below, sc blo in each of the next 3 sts, turn.

Rows 4–5 form Double Posts and Ridges st pat rep.

HERRINGBONE CABLE STITCH PATTERN

Worked in Rugged Rover
(see page 14)

Multiple of 2 sts + 5 sts
(also add 1 ch for base ch)

▌ *Featured Stitches*

Chain (ch)

Chain-space (ch-sp)

Front post treble crochet (FPTR)... *see page 77*

Single crochet (sc)

Treble (tr)

▌ *Instructions*

Foundation Row: Sc in 2nd ch from hook (count as st) and each ch to end, turn.

Row 2 (WS): Ch 1 (do not count as st), sc in first and each st to end, turn.

Row 3: Ch 1 (do not count as st), sc in each of first 3 sts, *ch 1, sk next st, sc in next st*, rep from * to * to end, turn.

Row 4: Ch 1 (do not count as st), sc in first and each sc and ch-sp to end, turn.

Row 5: Ch 1 (do not count as st), insert hook in first st, YO, draw loop through, leave these two lps on hook, working in front tr in first skipped st in row below (4th st from edge, tr will be diagonal), leaving last loop of tr on hook, YO, draw yarn through all 3 lps on hook (fig. 42), in previous row do not sk sc behind tr just made, *sc in next st, tr in next skipped st in row below (fig. 43), sk sc behind tr just made*, rep from * to * across to last 4 sts, sc in each st to end, turn.

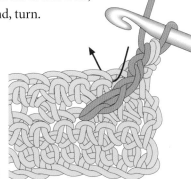

FIG. 42

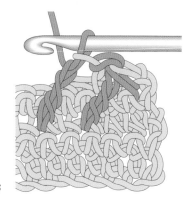

FIG. 43

Row 6: Ch 1 (do not count as st), sc in each of first 2 sts, *ch 1, sk next sc, sc in next st*, rep from * to * across to last st, sc in last st, turn.

Row 7: Ch 1 (do not count as st), sc in first 2 sts, sc in next ch-sp in previous row, FPTR around first tr in row below, *sc in next ch-sp in previous row, FPTR around next tr in row below*, rep from * to * across to last st, sc in last st, turn.

Rows 2–7 form Herringbone Cable st pat rep.

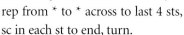

HONEYCOMB STITCH PATTERN

Worked in Scottish Reel
(see page 58)

Multiple of 6 sts + 2 sts
(also add 1 ch for base ch)

▌ *Featured Stitches*

Chain (ch)

Chain-space (ch-sp)

Post stitch cross (cr2) .... *see page 80*

Single crochet (sc)

Twist left (TWL)................. *see page 79*

Twist right (TWR)................ *see page 78*

▌ *Instructions*

Foundation Row: Sc in 2nd ch from hook (count as st) and each ch to end, turn.

Row 2: Ch 1 (do not count as st), sc in each of first 2 sts, *ch 1, sk next st, sc in each of next 2 sts*, rep from * to * to end, turn.

Row 3: Ch 1 (do not count as st), sc in each of first 2 sts, sc around first ch-sp, dc in first skipped sc in row below (below ch-sp just worked), dc in next skipped sc (3rd st to left) in row below, sk 2 sc behind 2 dc just made, sc around next ch-sp, sc in each of next 2 sc, *sc around next ch-sp, dc in next skipped st in row below (below ch-sp just worked), dc in next skipped st (3rd st to left) in row below, sk 2 sc behind 2 dc just made, sc around next ch-sp, sc in each of next 2 sc*, rep from * to * to end, turn.

Rows 4, 6, 8, and 10: Ch 1 (do not count as st), sc in first and each st to end, turn.

Row 5: Ch 1 (do not count as st), sc in each of first 2 sts, *cr2 over next 4 sts, sc in each of next 2 sts*, rep from * to * to end, turn.

Row 7: Ch 1 (do not count as st), sc in first st, *TWR over next 2 sts, sc in each of next 2 sts, TWL over next 2 sts*, rep from * to * across to last st, sc in last st, turn.

Row 9: Ch 1 (do not count as st), sc in first st, TWL over next 2 sts, *sc in each of next 2 sts, cr2 over next 4 sts*, rep from * to * across to last 5 sts, sc in each of next 2 sts, TWR over next 2 sts, sc in last st, turn.

Row 11: Ch 1 (do not count as st), *sc in each of next 2 sts, TWL over next 2 sts, TWR over next 2 sts (see fig. 38 on page 80)*, rep from * to * across to last 2 sts, sc in each of last 2 sts, turn.

Rows 4–11 form Honeycomb st pat rep.

INTERLOCKING DIAMONDS PANEL
Worked in Cottage Wear
(see page 32)
Worked over 20 sts
(add 1 ch for base ch)

▌ *Featured Stitches*
Chain (ch)
Front post double crochet (FPDC) .. *see page 77*
Post stitch cross (cr2) . . . . *see page 80*
Single crochet (sc)
Twist left (TWL) . . . . *see page 79*
Twist right (TWR) . . . . *see page 80*

▌ *Instructions*

Foundation Row: Sc in 2nd ch from hook and in each ch to end, turn.

Row 2 and All WS Rows: Ch 1 (do not count as st), sc in first and each st to end, turn.

Row 3 (RS): Ch 1 (do not count as st), sc in each of first 3 sts, FPDC around next st in row below (4th st from edge), sc in each of next 4 sts, FPDC around next st in row below, sc in each of next 2 sts, FPDC around next st in row below, sc in each of next 4 sts, FPDC around next st in row below, sc in each of last 3 sts, turn.

Row 5: Ch 1 (do not count as st), sc in each of first 3 sts, TWL over next 2 sts, sc in each of next 3 sts, TWL over next 2 sts, TWR over next 2 sts (see fig. 38 on page 80), sc in each of next 3 sts, TWR over next 2 sts, sc in each of last 3 sts, turn.

Row 7: Ch 1 (do not count as st), sc in each of first 4 sts, TWL over next 2 sts, sc in each of next 2 sts, cr2 over next 4 sts, sc in each of next 2 sts, TWR over next 2 sts, sc in each of last 4 sts, turn.

Row 9: Ch 1 (do not count as st), sc in each of first 5 sts, TWL over next 2 sts, TWR over next 2 sts, sc in each of next 2 sts, TWL over next 2 sts, TWR over next 2 sts, sc in each of last 5 sts, turn.

Row 11: Ch 1 (do not count as st), sc in each of first 5 sts, cr2 over next 4 sts, sc in each of next 2 sts, cr2 over next 4 sts, sc in each of last 5 sts, turn.

Row 13: Ch 1 (do not count as st), sc in each of first 4 sts, TWR over next 2 sts, sc in each of next 2 sts, TWL over next 2 sts, TWR over next 2 sts, sc in each of next 2 sts, TWL over next 2 sts, sc in each of last 4 sts, turn.

Row 15: Ch 1 (do not count as st), sc in each of first 3 sts, TWR over next 2 sts, sc in each of next 3 sts, cr2 over next 4 sts, sc in each of next 3 sts, TWL over next 2 sts, sc in each of last 3 sts, turn.

Row 17: Ch 1 (do not count as st), sc in each of first 2 sts, TWR over next 2 sts, sc in each of next 3 sts, TWR over next 2 sts, sc in each of next 2 sts, TWL over next 2 sts, sc in each of next 3 sts, TWL over next 2 sts, sc in each of last 2 sts, turn.

Row 19: Ch 1 (do not count as st), sc in each of first 2 sts, TWL over next 2 sts, sc in each of next 3 sts, TWL over next 2 sts, sc in each of next 2 sts, TWR over next 2 sts, sc in each of next 3 sts, TWR over next 2 sts, sc in each of last 2 sts, turn.

Rows 4–19 form Interlocking Diamonds panel rep.

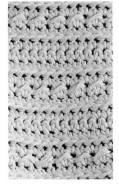

MOCK CABLE BORDER, EDGING, AND STITCH PATTERN

Worked in Dusty Miller, Scottish Reel, and Summer Solstice
(see pages 20, 58, and 68)
Multiple of 2 sts + 1 st
(also add 1 ch for base ch)

▌ *Featured Stitches*

Chain (ch)
Half double crochet (hdc)
Single crochet (sc)
Slip stitch (sl st)

▌ *Instructions*

Foundation Row: Sc in 2nd ch from hk (count as st) and in each ch to end, turn.

Rows 2, 4, 6, and 8 (RS): Ch 1 (do not count as st), sc in first and each st to end, turn.

Row 3: Ch 1 (do not count as st), sl st **loosely** in first and each st to end, turn.

Row 5: Ch 1 (do not count as st), sc in first st, *hdc in next st, sl st in next st*, rep from * to * across to last 2 sts, hdc in next st, sc in last st, turn.

Row 7: Ch 1 (do not count as st), sl st **loosely** in first st and each st to end, turn.

Row 9: Ch 1 (do not count as st), sc in first and each st to end, turn.

Rows 2-9 form Mock Cable st pat rep for Dusty Miller and Summer Solstice.

Rows 2-8 form Mock Cable Border for Scottish Reel.

Rows 2-7: form Mock Cable Border for Summer Solstice.

PLAITED CABLE PANEL

Worked in Celtic Challenge
(see page 40)
Worked over 12 sts
(add 1 ch for base ch)
Work over 9 sts if placed mid-row

Note: To repeat the panel across a row, do not work the stitches from † to † in rows 3 and 5 after making the first panel.

▌ *Featured Stitches*

Chain (ch)
Front post double crochet (FPDC).. *see page 77*
Single crochet (sc)

▌ *Instructions*

Foundation Row: Ch 1 (do not count as st), sc in first and each st to end, turn.

Row 2 and All WS Rows: Ch 1 (do not count as st), sc in first and each st to end, turn.

Row 3 (RS): Ch 1 (do not count as st), sc in first st, †FPDC around next st in row below, sc in each of next 2 sts†, FPDC around each of next 4 sts in row below, sc in each of next 2 sts, FPDC around next st in row below, sc in last st, turn.

Row 5: Ch 1 (do not count as st), sc in first st, †FPDC around FPDC in row below, sc in each of next 2 sts†, cb4 over next 4 sts, sc in each of next 2 sts, FPDC around next st in row below, sc in last st, turn.

Rows 2–5 form Plaited Cable panel rep.

ROPE DIAMOND PANEL

Worked in Ivy League
(see page 26)
Worked over 12 sts
(add 1 ch for base ch)

▌ *Featured Stitches*

Two-stitch cable (cb2) . . . . *see page 78*
Chain (ch)
Double crochet (dc)
Front post double crochet (FPDC). . *see page 77*
Front post treble crochet (FPTR). . . *see page 77*
Single crochet (sc)
Twist left (TWL). . . . . *see page 79*
Twist right (TWR). . . . . *see page 80*

▌ *Instructions*

Foundation Row: Sc in 2nd ch from hook (count as st) and in each ch to end, turn.

Row 2 (RS): Ch 1 (do not count as st), sc in each of first 6 sts, ch 1, sk next st, sc in each of next 5 sts, turn.

Row 3 and All WS Rows: Ch 1 (do not count as st), sc in first and each sc and ch-sp to end, turn.

Row 4: Ch 1 (do not count as st), sc in each of first 4 sts, working in front of work make 4 dc in skipped st from row 2, in previous row sk st behind 4 dc just made, sc in each of next 4 sts, turn.

Row 6: Ch 1 (do not count as st), sc in each of first 3 sts, TWR over next 2 sts, cb2 over next 2 dc, TWL over next 2 sts, sc in each of next 3 sts, turn.

Row 8: Ch 1 (do not count as st), sc in each of first 2 sts, TWR over next 2 sts, sc in next st, cb2, sc in next st, TWL over next 2 sts, sc in each of next 2 sts, turn.

Row 10: Ch 1 (do not count as st), sc in first st, TWR over next 2 sts, sc in each of next 2 sts, cb2, sc in each of next 2 sts, TWL over next 2 sts, sc in next st, turn.

Row 12: Ch 1 (do not count as st), sc in first st, TWL over next 2 sts, sc in each of next 2 sts, cb2, sc in each of next 2 sts, TWR over next 2 sts, sc in next st, turn.

Row 14: Ch 1 (do not count as st), sc in each of first 2 sts, TWL over next 2 sts, sc in next st, cb2, sc in next st, TWR over next 2 sts, sc in each of next 2 sts, turn.

Row 16: Ch 1 (do not count as st), sc in each of first 3 sts, TWL over next 2 sts, cb2, TWR over next 2 sts, sc in each of next 3 sts, turn.

Row 18: Ch 1 (do not count as st), sc in each of first 4 sts, sk next 3 FPDC, FPTR around next FPDC, sc in each of next 2 sc, working in front of FPTR just made FPTR around first skipped FPDC, sc in each of next 4 sts, turn.

Row 19: Ch 1 (do not count as st), sc in first and each st to end, turn.

Row 20: Ch 1 (do not count as st), sc in each of first 3 sts, TWR over next 2 sts, FPDC around 2nd sc in row below, FPDC around skipped (first) sc in row below, TWL over next 2 sts, sc in each of next 3 sts, turn.

Rows 7–20 form Rope Diamond panel rep.

SINGLE WEAVE STITCH PATTERN

Worked in Summer Solstice
(see page 68)
Multiple of 2 sts + 1 st
(also add 1 ch for base ch)

▌ *Featured Stitches*

Chain (ch)
Single crochet (sc)
Spike single crochet (ssc) . . . . *see page 74*

▌ *Instructions*

Foundation Row: Sc in 2nd ch from hook (count as st) and each ch to end, turn.

Row 2 (RS): Ch 1 (do not count as st), sc in first st, *ch 1, sk next st, sc in next st*, rep from * to * to end, turn.

Row 3: Ch 1 (do not count as st), sc in first st, * sc in skipped st in row below by working around previous row (ssc made, see page 74), ch 1, sk next sc*, rep from * to * across to last 2 sts, ssc in next (skipped) sc in row below, sc in last st, turn.

Row 4: Ch 1 (do not count as st), sc in first st, *ch 1, sk next ssc, ssc in next (skipped) sc in row below*, rep from * to * across to last 2 sts, ch 1, sk next ssc, sc in last st, turn.

Row 5: Ch 1 (do not count as st), sc in first st, *ssc in next (skipped) ssc in row below, ch 1, sk next ssc*, rep from * to * across to last 2 sts, ssc in next ssc in row below, sc in last st, turn.

Rows 4–5 form Single Weave st pat rep.

Work to desired length, ending with row 5 completed, then work Finishing Row.

Finishing Row (RS): Ch 1 (do not count as st), sc in each of first 2 sts, *ssc in next ssc in row below, sc in next ssc in previous row*, rep from * to * across to last st, sc in last st, turn.

TWO-ROW CABLE STITCH PATTERN

Worked in Ivy League
(see page 26)
Multiple of 5 sts
(add 1 ch for base ch)

▌ *Featured Stitches*

Three-stitch cable (cb3). . . . .*see page 78*
Chain (ch)
Double crochet (dc)
Front post double crochet (FPDC). .*see page 77*
Single crochet (sc)

▌ *Instructions*

Foundation Row: Sc in 2nd ch from hook (count as st) and each ch to end, turn.

Row 2 (RS): Ch 1 (do not count as st), sc in each of first 2 sts, ch 1, sk next st, sc in each of next 2 sts, *sc in each of next 2 sts, ch 1, sk next st, sc in each of next 2 sts*, rep from * to * to end, turn.

Row 3: Ch 1 (do not count as st), sc in first and each st to end, turn.

Row 4: Ch 1 (do not count as st), sc in first st, working in front of work make 3 dc in skipped st in row below, in previous row sk 3 sts behind dc just worked, *sc in next sc, working in front of work make 3 dc in skipped st in row below, sk 3 sc behind 3 dc just made, sc in next st*, rep from * to * to end, turn.

Row 5: Ch 1 (do not count as st), sc in first and each st to end, turn.

Row 6: Ch 1 (do not count as st), sc in first st, cb3 over next 3 sts, sc in next st, *sc in next st, cb3 over next 3 sts, sc in next st*, rep from * to * to end, turn.

Rows 5–6 form Two-Row Cable st pat rep.

Work to desired length, ending with row 5 completed, then work Finishing Row.

Finishing Row (RS): Ch 1 (do not count as st), sc in each of first 2 sts, FPDC around next FPDC in row below leaving last 2 lps on hook, *YO, insert hook around next FPDC in row below, draw up lp, YO, draw through 2 lps on hook (fig. 44)*, rep from * to * once more, YO (fig. 45), draw through all lps on hook (FPDC3tog made), in previous row sk only 1 st behind FPDC3tog just made, sc in each of next 2 sts, **sc in first 2 sts, FPDC3tog, in previous row sk only 1 st behind FPDC3tog just made, sc in each of next 2 sts**, rep from ** to ** to end, turn.

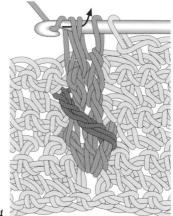

FIG. 44

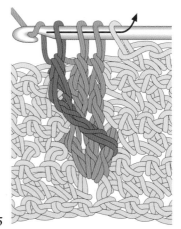

FIG. 45

89

VERTICAL POSTS STITCH PATTERN

Worked in Scottish Reel
(see page 58)
Multiple of 3 sts + 3 sts
(also add 1 ch for base ch)

Featured Stitches

Chain (ch)
Front post double crochet (FPDC)..*see page 77*
Single crochet (sc)

Instructions

Foundation Row: Sc in 2nd ch from hook and each ch to end, turn.

Row 2 (WS): Ch 1 (do not count as st), sc in each st to end, turn.

Row 3: Ch 1 (do not count as st), sc in first st, FPDC around next sc in row below, *sc in each of next 2 sts, FPDC around next sc in row below*, rep from * to * across to last st, sc in last st, turn.

Row 4: Ch 1 (do not count as st), sc in first and each st to end, turn.

Row 5: Ch 1 (do not count as st), sc in first st, FPDC around next FPDC in row below, *sc in each of next 2 sts, FPDC around next FPDC in row below*, rep from * to * across to last st, sc in last st, turn.

Rows 4–5 form Vertical Posts st pat rep.

WINDING ROAD PANEL

Worked in Celtic Challenge
(see page 40)
Worked over 8 sts
(add 1 ch for base ch)

Featured Stitches

Chain (ch)
Double crochet (dc)
Front post double crochet (FPDC)..*see page 77*
Single crochet (sc)

Instructions

Foundation Row: Sc in 2nd ch from hook (count as st) and in each ch to end, turn.

Row 2 (WS): Ch 1 (do not count as st), sc in first and each st to end, turn.

Row 3: Ch 1 (do not count as st), sc in first st, FPDC around each of next 2 sc in row below (2nd and 3rd sts from edge), sc in each of next 5 sc, turn.

Row 4: Ch 1 (do not count as st), sc in each of first 2 sc, dc in next st leaving 2 lps on hook, dc in same st leaving 3 lps on hook, dc in same st leaving 4 lps on hook, close with YO and pull through all lps on hook (bobble made, see page 75), sc in each of next 5 sc, turn.

Row 5: Ch 1 (do not count as st), sc in each of first 2 sts, FPDC around each of next 2 FPDC in row below, sc in each of next 4 sc, turn.

Rows 6, 8, 10, 14, 16, and 18: Ch 1 (do not count as st), sc in first and each st to end, turn.

Row 7: Ch 1 (do not count as st), sc in first 3 sts, FPDC around each of next 2 FPDC in row below, sc in each of next 3 sc, turn.

Row 9: Ch 1 (do not count as st), sc in first 4 sts, FPDC around each of next 2 FPDC in row below, sc in each of next 2 sc, turn.

Row 11: Ch 1 (do not count as st), sc in first 5 sts, FPDC around each of next 2 FPDC in row below, sc in next sc, turn.

Row 12: Ch 1 (do not count as st), sc in first 5 sts, bobble in next st, sc in each of next 2 sts, turn.

Row 13: Ch 1 (do not count as st), sc in first 4 sts, FPDC around each of next 2 FPDC in row below (diagonal posts made), sc in each of next 2 sc, turn.

Row 15: Ch 1 (do not count as st), sc in first 3 sts, FPDC around each of next 2 FPDC in row below, sc in each of next 3 sc, turn.

Row 17: Ch 1 (do not count as st), sc in first 2 sts, FPDC around each of next 2 FPDC in row below, sc in each of next 4 sc, turn.

Row 19: Ch 1 (do not count as st), sc in first st, FPDC around each of next 2 FPDC in row below, sc in each of next 5 sc, turn.

Rows 4–19 form Winding Road panel rep.

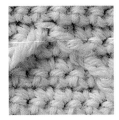

ZIGZAG POSTS STITCH PATTERN

Worked in Dusty Miller
(see page 20)

Multiple of 8 sts + 3 sts
(also add 1 ch for base ch)

▌ *Featured Stitches*

Chain (ch)

Chain-space (ch-sp)

Front post treble crochet (FPTR)... *see page 77*

Single crochet (sc)

Treble crochet (tr)

▌ *Instructions*

Foundation Row: Sc in 2nd ch from hook (count as st) and in each ch to end, turn.

Row 2 (RS): Ch 1 (do not count as st), sc in first st, *ch 1, sk next st, sc in each of next 7 sts*, rep from * to * across to last 2 sts, ch 1, sk next st, sc in last st, turn.

Row 3: Ch 1 (do not count as st), sc in first and each sc and ch-sp to end of row, turn.

Row 4: Ch 1 (do not count as st), sc in each of first 3 sts, working in front of crocheted fabric and working diagonally tr in first skipped st of row, *sc in each of next 3 sts, working in front of crocheted fabric tr in next skipped st of row 2, sc in each of next 3 sts, tr in same skipped st of row 2 as tr just worked*, rep from * to * across to last 7 sts, sc in each of next 3 sts, working in front of crocheted fabric tr in next skipped st of row 2, sc in each of last 3 sts, turn.

Row 5: Ch 1 (do not count as st), sc in first and each st to end, turn.

Row 6: Ch 1 (do not count as st), sc in each of first 5 sts, FPTR around first tr of row 4 leaving last 2 lps on hook (fig. 46), FPTR around next tr of row 4 and with last YO draw lp through last 3 lps on hook (fig. 47) (only sk 1 sc behind 2nd FPTR just made), *sc in each of next 7 sts, FPTR around next unworked tr of row 4 leaving last 2 lps on hook, FPTR around next tr of row 4 and with last YO draw lp through last 3 lps on hook (only sk 1 sc behind 2 FPTR just made)*, rep from * to * across to last 5 sts, sc in each of last 5 sts, turn.

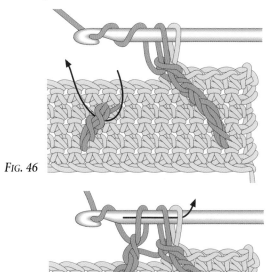

FIG. 46

FIG. 47

Row 7: Ch 1 (do not count as st), sc in first and each st to end, turn.

Rows 2–7 form Zigzag Posts st pat rep.

Finishing Techniques

After all the hard work and precious hours that you put into making sweater pieces, it's important to pay attention to the final details. It's the little things, like the seams, that often dramatically improve the finished appearance of the garment. Here are some helpful techniques.

DAMP BLOCKING

Don't automatically block your work. The characteristics of some yarns change when blocked. Patons *Classic Wool*, for example, relaxes substantially. If you're worried about disappointing results, wash and block your gauge swatch before tackling the garment pieces.

If the edges of your crocheted fabric don't curl or aren't stretched out of shape, you might not want to block the crocheted pieces before assembly.

It's best to block again after the cardigan, pullover, or vest is completely finished. This helps seams and added pieces, such as bands, lie flat.

1 Place the crocheted piece or finished garment on a towel. Using rustproof pins, attach the work to the towel to match the measurements on the schematics.

2 Place damp towels on top of the crocheted work, or mist it with water. Let dry before removing pins.

SEAMING

Aran sweaters have a lot of texture so it's best to use a seaming method that keeps bulk to a minimum. A mattress stitch or simple whipstitch is most suitable. Make both of these seams with the right sides out. This way you can choose where to insert the needle rather than hoping the seam is acceptable when the work is turned right side out. It's easier to make a neat seam, plus you can avoid working raised texture stitches into the seam.

Mattress Stitch

This is a sturdy stitch worked with both pieces right side up.

1 Place garment pieces side by side with edges matching row for row or stitch for stitch as possible. Thread a length of yarn on a blunt-tip tapestry needle.

2 Pull the needle and yarn from back to front through the lowest row (or stitch) of one crocheted edge. Leave a 6" yarn end for weaving into the wrong side of the work.

3 At the corresponding position on the opposite edge, pull the needle from front to back through the crocheted fabric.

4 Move up one row (or stitch) on the same edge and insert the needle through the crocheted fabric from back to front (fig. 48).

FIG. 48

5 On the opposite edge, insert the needle from front to back in the most recently worked row (or stitch).

6 Continue moving up the length of the edges in this manner, repeating steps 4–5. At the end of the edges, weave the seaming yarn strand back and forth through several loops on the wrong side of the work and then cut the strand.

Whipstitch (Overcast Stitch)

Most of the seams for the sweaters shown in this book were whipstitched.

1 Pin together the garment pieces, matching row for row or stitch for stitch as possible.

2 Pull a length of yarn on a blunt-tip tapestry needle from back to front through the bottom of one of the pieces. Leave a 6" yarn end.

3 Bring the yarn over the matched edges, move up a row or stitch, and again pull the needle through the work from front to back. Tug on the yarn until the crocheted edges are beside each other but not overlapped (fig. 49).

FIG. 49

4 Continue moving up the length of the edges in this manner. At the ends of the edges, weave the seaming yarn back and forth through several loops on the wrong side of the work and then cut it.

INSERTING SLEEVES

Whenever possible, sleeves are sewn into the armhole after adding the collar and bands for the bottom, front, and neck. Stitching additional pieces to the garment after inserting the sleeves is like wrestling an octopus.

Round Sleeve Assembly

Use this method when the top of the sleeve is shaped.

1 Join the shoulder and sides of the body pieces.

2 On one sleeve, sew together the long underarm edges.

3 Fold the sleeve lengthwise with the underarm seam at one edge. Place a stitch marker on the top edge of the sleeve, at the fold.

4 Pin a sleeve in an armhole with the underarm seam matching the side seam, and the marker on the sleeve cap matching the shoulder seam. Sew as pinned.

Flat Sleeve Assembly

This method is a good choice when the top of the sleeve is flat.

1 Join the back and front at one shoulder seam and then stitch the neckband or collar.

2 Place a stitch marker the specified distance from the shoulder seam on the back and front edges.

3 Fold the sleeve in half lengthwise and place a stitch marker on the top edge at the fold.

4 Spread the joined back and front, right side up, on a table. Place the wider (cap) end of a sleeve, also right side up, between the markers on one side of the body. Match the shoulder seam to the marker on the sleeve edge (fig. 50).

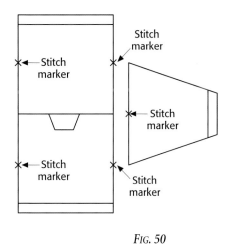

FIG. 50

5 Sew the sleeve.

6 Attach the remaining sleeve in the same manner.

7 Remove the markers. Refold the body and sleeves, aligning all matching edges. Join back to front by sewing up one side of the body, along the sleeve underarm, and to the end of the cuff. Join the remaining side of the body in the same manner.

Yarn Directory

Aran sweaters are all about luxurious, rich stitch patterns. Nevertheless, as you can see by looking at the projects in this book, color and content also have their place. In fact, the yarns recommended for the sweaters in this book were chosen to best showcase the textured stitches in each design. All of the yarns have similar weights but there's a wide range of content since this affects the mood of the design. "Rugged Rover," for example, is made from a denser wool for outdoor style. "Summer Solstice," on the other hand, looks dressier and is intended for warm weather because it's stitched with a lighter-twist cotton.

To achieve the best results, it's best to use the yarns suggested in the pattern that you're making. Once you have mastered the techniques, there is room for experimenting. You will be able to use almost any worsted or Aran-weight yarn and combine any of the stitch patterns in Crocheted Aran Sweaters *without wasting time trying to establish compatible gauges as you work a variety of stitches and patterns across a row. You can also try stitching any featured sweater with any other yarn in the book.*

Briggs and Little *Heritage*; 100% wool; 4 oz./113g; 215 yds./196 m; featured in **Rugged Rover** *(see page 14)*

Cascade *Sierra*; 80% cotton, 20% wool; 3½ oz./100g; 190 yds./173 m; featured in **Summer Solstice** *(see page 68)*

Lion Brand *Wool-Ease*; 80% acrylic, 20% wool; 3 oz./85g; 197 yds./180 m; featured in **Dusty Miller** *(see page 20)*

Patons *Decor*; 75% acrylic, 25% wool; 3½ oz./100g; 210 yds./192 m; featured in **Forever Diamonds** *(see page 53)*

I am grateful to the many yarn manufacturers and distributers who generously provided yarn so that my designs could come to life. The support and encouragement of these companies is appreciated. A special thank you to Gayle Bunn at Patons/Spinrite; Ingrid Skacel at Skacel Collection, Inc.; Josie Dolan at S. R. Kertzer Limited; John Little at Briggs & Little Woolen Mills Ltd.; Uyvonne Bigham at Plymouth Yarn Company; Joan Somerville at Cascade Yarns Inc.; and the helpful staff at Lion Brand Yarn Company.

—*Jane Snedden Peever*

BRIGGS & LITTLE WOOLEN MILLS LTD.

3500 Route 635
Harvey, York County, NB
Canada E6K 1J8

Telephone: *(800) 561-9276*

Web site:
www.briggsandlittle.com

E-mail:
woolyarn@nb.sympatico.ca

CASCADE YARNS INC.

PO Box 58168
Tukwila, WA 98138

Telephone: *(800) 548-1048*

Web site:
www.cascadeyarns.com

E-mail:
sales@cascadeyarns.com

LION BRAND YARN COMPANY

34 West 15th Street
New York, NY 10011

Telephone: *(800) 258-276*

Web site: www.lionbrand.com

E-mail: *customerservice@ lionbrandyarn.com*

PATONS

PO Box 40
Listowel, ON
Canada N4W 3H3

Telephone: *(888) 858-4258*

Web site:
www.patonsyarns.com

PLYMOUTH YARN COMPANY

PO Box 28
Bristol, PA 19007

Telephone: *(800) 523-8932*

Web site:
www.plymouthyarn.com

E-mail:
pyc@plymouthyarn.com

S. R. KERTZER LIMITED

105a Winges Road
Woodbridge, ON
Canada L4L 6C2

Telephone: *(800) 263-2354*

Web site:
www.kertzer.com

E-mail:
info@kertzer.com

SKACEL COLLECTION, INC.

PO Box 88110
Seattle, WA 98138

Telephone: *(800) 255-1278*

Web site:
www.skacelknitting.com

E-mail:
info@skacelknitting.com

Patons *Classic Wool*; 100% wool; 3½ oz./100g; 223 yds./204 m; featured in **Cottage Wear** *(see page 32)*

Plymouth *Encore*; 75% acrylic, 25% wool; 3½ oz./100g; 200 yds./182 m; featured in **Morning Mist** *(see page 8)* and **Scottish Reel** *(see page 58)*

Plymouth *Galway Highland Heather*; 100% wool; 3½ oz./100g; 210 yds./192 m; featured in **Green Mantle** *(see page 48)*

Skacel *Snow Goose*; 80% acrylic, 20% wool; 14 oz./400g; 940 yds./850 m; featured in **Ivy League** *(see page 26)*

Stylecraft *Special Aran with Wool*; 80% acrylic, 20% wool; 14 oz./400g; 940 yds./850 m; featured in **Celtic Challenge** *(see page 40)*

Meet the Author

Jane Snedden Peever is a rare talent. She has an instinctive understanding of stitch patterns, which allows her to create innovative Aran pattern work for crocheters. Where others may falter with a pattern or reach for pen and paper to work out details, Jane just keeps on stitching. Her natural abilities, which surfaced when she was a youngster, were nurtured by her mother. Soon Jane was digging into one complex pattern after another, the hook still warm as she started the base chain for the newest sweater. Challenge motivates her. Nevertheless, the direction of Jane's design work is less complex.

"I like to use simple repeats that aren't hard to remember and I prefer to use the basic stitches but combine them in different ways. I want my designs to be attainable: something the average crocheter could attempt and finish within a reasonable amount of time. It's a real challenge to take simple stitches and work them into unique but wearable designs," she explains.

An inventor at heart, Jane loves to play with new ideas and concepts to create something unique. She doesn't like doing anything twice and claims she has a short attention span.

Upon graduation from university, Jane's passion for stitching overwhelmed her desire to do much else. She spent some years in her chosen field before heeding the siren call of the hook. Soon she had her own yarn shop in Ontario, Canada.

These days, Jane divides her time between designing for yarn manufacturers and raising her two energetic children. Her work debuted in book form as several featured garments in *Crocheted Sweaters: Simple Stitches, Great Designs*, published in 2001.

Jane lives in Pembroke, Ontario, Canada, with her husband, Todd, and their children, Tessa and Thomas. She would love to hear from crocheters. Her e-mail address is tjpeever@nrtco.net.